DISASTER AND THE POLITICS OF INTERVENTION

The Columbia University Press and Social Science Research Council
Series on the Privatization of Risk

THE COLUMBIA UNIVERSITY PRESS AND SOCIAL SCIENCE RESEARCH COUNCIL SERIES ON THE PRIVATIZATION OF RISK

Edited by Craig Calhoun and Jacob S. Hacker

The early twenty-first century is witnessing a concerted effort to privatize risk—to shift responsibility for the management or mitigation of key risks onto private-sector organizations or directly onto individuals. This series uses social science research to analyze this issue in depth. Each volume presents a concise review of a particular topic from the perspective of the public and private allocation of risk and responsibility and offers analysis and empirical, evidence-based opinion from leading scholars in the fields of economics, political science, sociology, anthropology, and law. Support for the series comes from the John D. and Catherine T. MacArthur Foundation.

Jacob S. Hacker, ed., *Health at Risk: America's Ailing Health System—and How to Heal It*

Donald W. Light, ed., *The Risks of Prescription Drugs*

Katherine S. Newman, ed., *Laid Off, Laid Low: Political and Economic Consequences of Employment Insecurity*

Mitchell A. Orenstein, ed., *Pensions, Social Security, and the Privatization of Risk*

Robert E. Wright, ed., *Bailouts: Public Money, Private Profit*

Disaster and the Politics of Intervention

EDITED BY ANDREW LAKOFF

COLUMBIA UNIVERSITY PRESS | NEW YORK

A COLUMBIA/SSRC BOOK

COLUMBIA UNIVERSITY PRESS
Publishers Since 1893
New York   Chichester, West Sussex

Copyright © 2010 The Social Science Research Council
All rights reserved

Library of Congress Cataloging-in-Publication Data

Disaster and the politics of intervention / edited by
Andrew Lakoff.
        p.   cm. — (The Columbia University Press
    and Social Science Research Council series on the
    privatization of risk)
    Includes bibliographical references.
      ISBN 978-0-231-14696-8 (cloth : alk. paper) —
    ISBN 978-0-231-14697-5 (pbk. : alk. paper) —
    ISBN 978-0-231-51925-0 (ebook)

      1. Disaster relief—Political aspects. 2. Disaster
    relief—Government policy. 3. Emergency management—
    Political aspects. 4. Emergency management—
    Government policy. 5. Intervention (Federal government)
    I. Lakoff, Andrew, 1970– II. Title. III. Series.

HV553.D548 2010
363.34'8—dc22

                                        2009049463

Design by Julie Fry
Cover by Vin Dang

CONTENTS

DISASTER AND THE POLITICS OF INTERVENTION

Introduction

ANDREW LAKOFF

It's laissez-faire until you get in deep shit.

—John Gutfreund, former CEO of Salomon Brothers[1]

In late October 2007, a series of wildfires raged uncontrollably in Southern California, surrounding the suburbs of Los Angeles and San Diego
and moving rapidly toward the urban core of San Diego. Over half a
million residents were evacuated from their homes, a federal emergency
was declared, the U.S. Marines and National Guard were mobilized,
and President Bush flew to the region to demonstrate the government's
commitment to those in need. A combustible mixture of gusting winds,
heat, and stores of dry brush was blamed for the conflagration. But as a
number of commentators noted, the magnitude of the disaster could not
be attributed solely to these forces of nature. The scale of the firestorm
also pointed to the San Diego region's failure to enact regulatory measures or devote public resources that would mitigate wildfire risk. The
region's politicians had been unwilling to implement zoning regulations
to stem rapid housing development into the parched backcountry where
fire risk was especially high. And San Diego voters had declined to fund
improvement to the city's strapped fire department, even in the wake
of catastrophic wildfires that had swept through San Diego County four
years earlier.

A relatively minor but telling episode during the 2007 fires pointed
to a central issue in this volume: the role of public-sector intervention

in mitigating the risk of catastrophe. As local firefighters, overwhelmed by the firestorm, awaited assistance from other regions, the "Wildfire Protection Unit" of American International Group Inc. (AIG) passed through barricades to protect specific properties in the wealthy northern suburbs of San Diego—those houses belonging to members of AIG's Private Client Group, for which membership cost an average of $19,000 per year. Whether the flames would destroy the homes of area residents thus potentially depended on how much they had paid for private insurance—a throwback to the nineteenth century, before governments took on the responsibility of firefighting in the United States.

AIG would, of course, become infamous a year later, when it found itself at the center of another conflagration. This time the disaster was far more widespread: a global financial crisis whose scale and catastrophic potential outstripped the worst scenarios envisioned by economic planners. The insurance giant's reckless entry into the under-regulated market for mortgage-backed securities was widely cited as one source of the financial system's calamitous failure. Analogies were made to the great crash of 1929. Some analysts suggested that the nation—and the world—was facing a period of economic decline that would rival the Great Depression. Government officials worked feverishly to assuage an anxious public and to enact regulatory reforms and stimulus measures to keep the financial firestorm from spreading. Soon after inheriting this crisis, newly inaugurated President Barack Obama warned that a failure to act boldly could "turn crisis into catastrophe."[2] But according to what norms would new regulations to protect against catastrophe be developed? And what kind of institution could be created that would have the power to monitor and intervene in potential financial disaster across the globe?

Such questions were salient across multiple domains—not only to the financial system, but also to environmental, health, and security risks. Indeed, the first decade of the twenty-first century was punctuated by a series of domestic and international emergencies, each of which challenged extant means of governmental intervention. To list a few of the most visible such events: the terrorist attacks of September 11, 2001, and the anthrax letters that followed; the 2004 tsunami that devastated huge areas of south and Southeast Asia; the flooding of New Orleans in the wake of Hurricane Katrina in 2005; and ongoing calamities, such as the intensifying AIDS pandemic in the global South and the brutal conflict in Darfur, that continued to provoke calls for urgent intervention.

These domestic and international emergencies of the new millennium were quite disparate in cause, geographic reach, and temporal frame. However, their juxtaposition highlights certain features of the contemporary politics of intervention into disaster. First, in each case the onset of an "emergency" situation made it possible to galvanize governmental response—whereas earlier proposals for preventive measures could not muster political support. Second, the perceived failures of governments to prevent or adequately prepare for these events generated their own political crises. In the case of Hurricane Katrina, for example, the Department of Homeland Security's slow and poorly organized response played a major role in the decline of the Bush administration's public legitimacy. And third, there were vocal disagreements among experts both over the appropriate measures for managing these emergencies and over the locus of responsibility for implementing such measures.

The issue of the management of catastrophic risk is linked to broader current debates over the relative roles of the state, the private sector, and non-governmental organizations (NGOs) in ensuring collective security. This volume seeks to contribute findings from recent social scientific research to such discussions. It is part of the Social Science Research Council's project on "The Privatization of Risk," led by Craig Calhoun and Jacob Hacker. The project considers the ways in which the distribution and management of collective risks has changed over recent decades. It analyzes the social and economic effects of efforts to replace public institutions with market mechanisms, shifting the burden of risk to those without substantial private wealth.

The term "disaster" does not connote a unified field of events. Just to take two examples from this volume: a catastrophic natural disaster and the prospect of global warming obviously call for different types of interventions, given their different scales and temporalities. An acute emergency demands immediate stabilization in a specific area, whereas the prospect of gradual—if calamitous—environmental transformation points toward prudent regulatory intervention on a global scale. However, juxtaposing these disparate kinds of events calls attention to the political stakes involved in understanding an event—or potential event—as a disaster.

There is a paradox inherent to the use of the term "disaster." On the one hand, it can bring public attention and resources to bear on a situation that "normal" circumstances cannot, even when such normalcy involves intense suffering. This has to do with the sense—from the old notion of an "act of God"—that a disaster could not have been avoided, that it was not foreseeable or preventable. Victims are not responsible for their suffering and thus are deserving of relief. On the other hand, since this attention and these resources are contingent on an acute temporality, the kinds of interventions implied by the notion of disaster are difficult to sustain in the long term.[3] It is hard to generate political will to act in advance to avoid or to mitigate the effects of disasters. One question for the politics of intervention, then, is whether there are ways to take advantage of the attention and resources that "disasters" (whether in the present, as in wildfires, or in the future, as in climate change) galvanize while designing political technologies that diminish vulnerability and are sustainable in the long term.

Over the course of the twentieth century, governments played an increasing role in the management of collective risks—whether from natural disasters, outbreaks of infectious disease, or economic downturns. However, the increasing complexity and interdependence of systems for sustaining collective well-being as well as the emergence of risks deriving from modern technologies themselves have exceeded the capacities of many of the risk management practices initially developed in the industrial era. Such modernization risks include climate change, mass casualty terrorist attacks, international financial crises, and novel infectious diseases that have emerged as a result of ecological transformation. The challenge to risk management comes both from the difficulty of assessing the probability of unprecedented events within frameworks based on statistical calculation and from the temporal and spatial extent of the consequences of such events. In this context, governments face renewed uncertainty over the appropriate political and technical measures to mitigate the risk of disaster. As the sociologist Ulrich Beck writes, "We live in a world that has to make decisions concerning its future under the conditions of manufactured, self-inflicted insecurity."[4]

The contributions to this volume focus on the political and technical challenges faced in governmental efforts to approach these new forms of catastrophic risk. The question is especially pressing in the case of threats whose probability is difficult or impossible to calculate, but whose consequences could be catastrophic. Such threats typically defy extant means of regulation both in terms of their incalculability and in terms of their scale. The essays ask how the category of catastrophic risk should be rethought in order to provide for more resilient critical systems and more sustainable practices of disaster management.

In her chapter, "Beyond Calculation: A Democratic Response to Risk," science studies scholar Sheila Jasanoff argues that contemporary catastrophic risks have escaped the control of technocratic managers and should be understood more broadly as a problem for democratic governance. She begins by noting a series of uncertainties that such risks raise for government: First, experts face analytic limits in assessing the impacts of potentially global catastrophes. Second, bureaucratic efforts to develop streamlined procedures elide the complexity of the settings in which such events take place. Third, the problem of responsibility is not easily settled: who should be protected and how should vulnerabilities be distributed? And finally, there is the question of how scarce resources for mitigation should be allocated. These issues indicate that adequate responses must be simultaneously technical and political. In response, Jasanoff advocates a form of democratic risk governance that is oriented not toward managerial control but toward building trust and transparency. She prescribes the development of "technologies of humility" that admit to the limits of expert calculation and thus are open to contribution from a public that has its own experiences and understandings of the potential for harm. Such technologies will, Jasanoff argues, be crucial to building resilience against future disasters.

An additional requirement for the governance of catastrophic risk is administrative durability. In the midst of crisis, political action may be galvanized, but in the absence of the event such urgency often fades. The struggle in the United States over the past three decades to define a coherent mission for and maintain a stable administrative apparatus of "emergency management" illustrates this difficulty. The roots of federal emergency management are in Cold War civil defense. Civil defense programs were initially designed to distribute responsibility across multiple levels of government: while the federal government played a coordinative role, local and regional agencies were expected to actively respond in the event of a nuclear attack.[5] During the 1960s and 1970s, the field of emergency management expanded to include preparedness for and response to natural disasters, such as floods, earthquakes, and wildfires. Founded in 1979, the Federal Emergency Management Agency (FEMA) was organized as a central node in a distributed network, with a coordinative rather than a command role with respect to local response agencies. However, there were downsides to merging different functions in a coordinative agency. Ensuring the collaborative operation of disparate entities—police and fire, public health, charities, and so forth—has been an ongoing challenge in organizing emergency response.

Moreover, the combined mission of emergency management has generated difficulties. As public administration scholar Patrick Roberts shows in his essay, "Private Choices, Public Harms: The Evolution of National Disaster Organizations in the United States," the tension between civil defense goals and the demand for natural disaster preparedness has been a continuous problem for federal emergency management. Roberts points out that the Department of Homeland Security's initial focus on terrorism prevention rather than "all hazards" preparedness was one source of its failure to respond adequately to Hurricane Katrina. Roberts argues that a key factor in creating a functioning emergency management apparatus at the federal level will be defining a coherent strategy for the Department of Homeland Security (DHS). He suggests that the DHS should focus its mission on preparedness for and response to multiple hazards rather than on terrorism prevention alone.

As Roberts notes, the Bush administration's use of contractors rather than government employees to provide public services, based on an ethos of market-driven solutions to public problems, hampered the DHS's ability to mount a coherent response to Hurricane Katrina. The scandal provoked by the failed response to Katrina indicates that, at least at the national level, there is agreement about the necessity of a strong governmental role in protecting against disaster.

However, whatever political consensus there is on the responsibility of the government for managing emergencies breaks down when the scale of response extends from the local and national to the global. On the one hand, global interconnection via circuits of communication and transportation means that the question of responsibility for managing disasters must be posed at a transnational scale. This is exemplified by the prominent role of the U.S. military, alongside philanthropic organizations and NGOs, in responding to humanitarian disasters, such as the Asian tsunami, refugee crises linked to military conflicts, and the global AIDS pandemic. On the other hand, it is unclear how lines of responsibility among these diverse organizations should be drawn. How should state and multilateral agencies govern events that do not easily fall into existing purviews—both of jurisdictional responsibility and of technical capacity?

The problems faced by domestic emergency management—such as the locus of responsibility for dealing with crises and the difficulty of engaging in sustained intervention—are heightened in a global context. As the recent global financial crisis illustrates, political and technical mechanisms for managing risks that outstrip national boundaries have not yet been established. Two chapters in this volume—one on complex humanitarian emergencies and the other on the global AIDS crisis—address the issue of developing measures to intervene in disasters taking place in settings in which the nation-state apparatus is either unable or unwilling to protect the welfare of its citizens. These chapters do not aim to denounce the global political and economic system in which such suffering is allowed to take place (though their authors might well take such a position if queried); rather they propose modest practical interventions to address specific needs.

Complex humanitarian disasters are situations characterized by massive political disruption and by the absence of functioning welfare institutions. In these situations, refugees from political violence face the combined scourges of physical dislocation, hunger, disease, and the threat of further violence. Non-governmental organizations and multilateral agencies have sought to fill the void of state protection to provide humanitarian relief—food, medicine, and shelter—to refugees. However, the intervention of these organizations is premised on the short duration of the emergency situation. They do not have the institutional mechanisms to secure the well-being of the population over the long term. And yet these seemingly acute emergencies whose source is political instability have become chronic in many parts of the world.[6]

Among the many problems that humanitarian NGOs face in approaching these situations of large-scale human suffering and violent conflict is the issue of providing security for their employees against armed attacks. Here we find another setting in which private-sector entities have substituted, in halting and often insufficient ways, for public agencies in mitigating disaster risk. In his chapter, "Strange Brew: Private Military Contractors and Humanitarians," security analyst P. W. Singer analyzes the increasing dependence of humanitarian NGOs on private military contractors to provide security in situations in which state-based military and police forces are either not present or ineffective. The central role played by private military firms in these settings—one mostly unacknowledged by humanitarian organizations—poses problems of accountability and responsibility. What rules should govern the actions of private military firms in such contexts? Singer argues that given their dependence on such arrangements for the foreseeable future, humanitarian NGOs must work to develop norms and protocols that can regulate these problematic interventions.

Philanthropic and multilateral responses to the global AIDS pandemic similarly raise questions of responsibility for managing emergency situations over an indefinite period. As it has intensified in the global South, the human suffering and social collapse caused by the pandemic have led to a medical humanitarian movement to provide access to antiretroviral drugs that would otherwise be unaffordable to patients. However, since the survival of HIV-positive patients requires the lifelong provision of medication, the long-term sustainability of this form of intervention is in question. This points in a stark way to the issue of the relation between the private and public sectors in responding to emergencies: at what moments, and in what ways, should intellectual property laws be suspended or rewritten to ensure that treatment can be offered in the event of public health emergencies?

As legal scholar Heinz Klug notes in his contribution to the volume, "Risking Health: HIV/AIDS and the Problem of Access to Essential Medicines," the market-based system in which advanced pharmaceuticals are developed and distributed is badly suited to the provision of long-term treatment for life-threatening disease in resource-poor settings. Meanwhile, the multilateral and philanthropic organizations that have sought to meet the demand for affordable drugs do not have the means to do so over the lifetimes of those suffering from the disease. Again, the temporality of emergency intervention—in this case, the provision of medication access—does not suffice for the provision of long-term welfare. In response to the AIDS crisis, Klug prescribes specific changes to intellectual property law that would enable the development of a generics industry that could provide the next-generation of therapies to poor countries that lack pharmaceutical production capacity. What Klug proposes is, then, the design of concrete and carefully targeted administrative techniques—in this case, a change in the legal regime—that could transform the modality of emergency intervention so that it is sustainable over the long term.

The threat of anthropogenic climate change obviously differs from these current humanitarian disasters in a number of ways, including the extent to which its impact has not yet been felt and indeed remains uncertain. Climate change is a potential disaster unfolding in slow motion. It shares with these other disasters, however, the problem of designing technical and political instruments that can extend across national boundaries and govern the actions of diverse institutional actors. Mitigating the risk of climate change would require transnational cooperation and the ability to regulate the activities of powerful private-sector actors. For these reasons, despite consensus among scientists on the danger, it remains profoundly difficult to build political consensus for a plan that could plausibly mitigate catastrophic risk.

The case of climate change thus raises the question of whether collective action across political boundaries can be generated in advance of an impending catastrophe. Are governments willing or able to make decisions that might sacrifice economic growth in the name of intervening in a potential disaster? And if not, are there ways to design technical interventions that are politically feasible—given that, for example, a carbon tax might not be? In his chapter, "Constructing Carbon Markets: Learning from Experiments in the Technopolitics of Emissions Trading Schemes," sociologist Donald MacKenzie addresses the question of how state agencies might forge market devices that would create incentives to effectively mitigate climate risks. MacKenzie analyzes how the technical and political challenges of dealing with greenhouse-gas emissions have been handled in the European Union's incipient carbon trading system.

Specifically, MacKenzie describes the operation of a "cap-and-trade" system, currently functioning in Europe and under consideration in the United States and elsewhere. Since the EU program is a possible model for the rest of the world, it is an important experiment in considering what it would take to implement such a system on a larger scale. The chapter points to the need to reflect carefully about how to construct an emissions market in order to increase its likelihood of success. MacKenzie shows that such success will hinge on specific details of market design: thus, for example, the decision on whether to initially give away or to auction emission credits will have an enormous impact on the eventual viability of a carbon trading market. More generally, from this analysis of the challenges involved in building a functioning cap-and-trade system, we can see the importance of careful reflection on the design of regulatory interventions.

In closing, it is worth pointing to the ways that the social scientific inquiries in this volume provide broader guidance about the appropriate role of government in the management of catastrophic risk. For the most part, the chapters to follow do not focus on removing the sources of risk; rather, they emphasize the design of mechanisms that can mitigate it. They propose practical approaches rather than overarching theoretical visions. To deal with current or impending disasters, they prescribe targeted interventions that, it is hoped, will be technically feasible and can work within existing political constraints. Despite this modesty of purpose, it is possible to glean from these contributions a more general set of guideposts for intervening in potential and actual disasters.

One insight that emerges from these chapters is that managing catastrophic risk will require the development of new regulatory norms and new organizational forms. For example, while it is clear that purely market-based approaches cannot be depended upon to provide collective health and security, it may be that market experiments in combination with government regulation can be part of a broad effort to create sustainable practices of collective security. Thus, for example, Klug proposes a flexible patent regime that is as much focused on the provision of medicines as a necessary part of public health as it is on ensuring that biomedical innovation is encouraged. And MacKenzie points toward the design of a carbon emissions trading scheme that has the potential to be both politically feasible and technically efficacious.

A more general suggestion about regulatory norms comes from the current response to the global financial crisis. The deregulation of the financial industry is widely blamed for inciting the spiral of events that has threatened the viability of the global financial system. While it remains to be seen precisely what this crisis will mean for the future role of government in managing catastrophic risk, one possibility is that the event will, retrospectively, be seen as the bookend on a period in which the "privatization of risk" was a dominant policy ideal. What norms are now being proposed in the wake of the apparent failure of deregulation? If there is agreement that a lack of regulation was one cause of the crisis, what principles will guide the enactment of new regulatory measures? And if there is also consensus that such regulations would have to extend beyond the boundaries of the nation-state, what global institutions will be charged with implementing and enforcing them?

A prime candidate for the target of new regulations is "systemic risk." This term alludes to the interdependence of the heterogeneous elements of a sociotechnical system. In the context of finance, it refers to the regulatory problem posed by the existence of firms whose failure could provoke a collapse of the entire system. The existence of such systemic risks, most political actors now agree, demands measures above and beyond existing ways of regulating finance. However, in the vision of reformers, such regulation should not fundamentally transform the structure of the system or even slow its functioning. Rather, it should provide the system with "resilience" against unexpected shocks. The salience of these terms — systemic risk as the target of regulation and resilience as its goal — can potentially be extended beyond the domain of finance into the other arenas of risk that are discussed in this volume: large-scale natural disasters, pandemic disease, climate change, and humanitarian emergency. From each chapter, one draws suggestions on the design of sustainable technical and political instruments that can help develop resilience against unexpected and potentially catastrophic events.

NOTES

1   Quoted in Michael Lewis, "The End," *Condé Nast Portfolio*, December 2008.

2   Brian Faler, "Obama Pushes Congress to Complete Stimulus Package," *Bloomberg News*, February 4, 2009.

3   Legal scholar Michele Landis has argued that the Great Depression was strategically constructed according to a "disaster narrative" in order to detach poverty from personal responsibility and thus justify government intervention within a liberal political tradition. This disaster narrative, she notes, had three elements: (1)

a calamitous event that could not be foreseen or prevented by those suffering from its impact, (2) a victim who is innocent and therefore deserving of help, and (3) a limited temporal duration of need (the misfortune is a temporary situation). Thus a number of dispersed, local effects of suffering were aggregated into a singular event in order to use federal disaster relief as a means to combat widespread poverty. Michele L. Landis, "Fate, Responsibility, and 'Natural' Disaster Relief: Narrating the American Welfare State," *Law and Society Review* 33, no. 2 (1999).

4   Ulrich Beck, *World at Risk* (Cambridge, UK: Polity Press, 2007), 8.

5   Stephen J. Collier and Andrew Lakoff, "Distributed Preparedness: The Spatial Logic of Domestic Security in the United States," *Environment and Planning D: Society and Space* 26, no. 1 (2008): 7–28.

6   Craig Calhoun, "The Imperative to Reduce Suffering: Charity, Progress, and Emergencies in the World of Humanitarian Action," in *Humanitarianism in Question: Politics, Power, Ethics*, ed. Michael Barnett and Thomas G. Weiss (Ithaca, NY: Cornell University Press, 2008).

CHAPTER ONE

Beyond Calculation |
A Democratic Response to Risk

SHEILA JASANOFF

Twice in the new millennium, in calamities barely eight months apart, first in Asia in December 2004 and again in the United States in August 2005, water played havoc with hundreds of thousands of human lives. The two disasters, a tidal wave (or tsunami, as the Japanese call it) and a hurricane, occurred worlds apart—spatially, socially, culturally, economically, in their apparent causes and impacts, and in the political and humanitarian responses that each evoked. But there were deep similarities as well. Both were catastrophic in scale, producing death, dislocation, and damage of unprecedented magnitude. Both were "natural" disasters, in that each originated in the workings of nature outside the bounds of human control, but both revealed the interactivity of the natural and the social in apportioning disaster's consequences. Both also drew attention to the fact that we often learn most about risk—who is at risk, for what reasons, and to what degree—only in hindsight, after risk transmutes into harm. Reflecting on what was like and unlike in these two events allows us to reevaluate how far we have come, as enlightened societies, in attempting to manage risks of global consequence. What techniques have our rulers evolved for predicting the ills that affect large numbers and cut across jurisdictions, and how effectively can experts' powers of prediction guard against harms that seem continually to befall the most vulnerable segments of humankind?

Like the other contributions to this volume, this chapter is about risk that, through its spatial scope, violence, or suddenness, overwhelms reason—in short, catastrophic risk—and our paradoxical attempts to cope with the irrational in rational terms. Whereas risk is normally seen as a property of the indeterminate future, an inexact but not incalculable foreshadowing of things to come, I will argue that risk is better conceived as an extrapolation ahead in time from misfortunes we already know, have experienced, or tried to master. In this respect, risk is a product of human imaginations disciplined and conditioned by an awareness of the past; put differently, risk is a disciplined projection of archived historical memory onto the blank screen of the future. That memory, however, is necessarily partial and selective: the past is not the same for everyone who experiences it, especially when interpreters are separated by divisions of status, income, and analytic capacity. As historians have shown us, the ruler's memory does not recall prior events in the same way as that of the subaltern; post-disaster litigation reveals that causes invariably look different from the standpoints of the victims and the originators of risky enterprises. Even science, modernity's most reliable identifier of causes, narrows the possible channels of explanation in the process of illuminating them.[1] It follows that, to enhance a society's capacity for understanding and controlling risk, we have to widen our analytic horizon to take in more than the sciences of prediction. We have to become better skilled at developing strategies of collective recall and at seeing risk itself not only as the narrow concern of "management" but—consistent with the wider message of this volume—as part of the wider political preserve of "governance."

I am not alone, of course, in seeing risk as memory bumped forward. To some degree, the entire enterprise of technical risk assessment arose from an ability to deploy history instrumentally, through gradually increasing sophistication with what the philosopher Ian Hacking has called the "taming of chance."[2] The future, as inhabitants of the twentieth century gradually recognized, was not deterministic but governed by probabilities. Chance itself, however, was often not random but amenable to more or less reliable forms of accounting, and knowledge of the past was crucial to the accuracy of many forecasts. Our ability to compile and manipulate large numbers grew. The actuarial tabulation of recurrent bad events, from common illnesses and disabilities to accidents and financial ruin, and the estimation from these aggregated numbers of likely risk in individual lives formed the basis of the insurance industry, one of modernity's signature social achievements. If in every life some harms must occur, then insurance promises that no one will have to face them alone and destitute, without any resources to compensate for injury and loss. Insurance spreads risk, equalizing to some extent the lot of the poor and vulnerable and the lot of the protected and rich.

The latter half of the twentieth century, however, gave rise to risks that escape the framework of actuarial prediction, in part because there is little or no direct historical experience to fall back on in evaluating them. Some threats are so infrequent, fantastical, slow to mature, spatially and temporally far-reaching, or causally complex that they are literally as well as figuratively incalculable; climate change, the product of centuries of industrialization, is but one example. Others arise through historically contingent human behaviors and human-environment interactions that no one, it seems, could have imagined, let alone foretold; fundamentalist religious terrorism and stratospheric ozone depletion can be cited as examples. Yet such risks may be catastrophic, at the level of individual as well as communal life. It is hard to date the precise moment of emergence of such incalculable risks, but a turning point may have been the explosion of the first nuclear weapon at the Trinity test site in the deserts of New Mexico on July 16, 1945. That initial public demonstration of the results of the Manhattan Project alerted the world to the possibility of total annihilation. It is said that, moments before the Trinity blast, the eminent physicist Enrico Fermi "began offering anyone listening a wager on 'whether or not the bomb would ignite the atmosphere, and if so, whether it would merely destroy New Mexico or destroy the world.'"[3] Since then, not only the continued threat of a nuclear holocaust but a succession of more or less devastating natural and human-made disasters have kept alive the specter of essentially incalculable, and hence uninsurable, risks.[4] How to govern these — not simply manage them — has emerged as one of the great technical, political, and ethical challenges of the early twenty-first century.

Most people tend to think of natural or technological disasters when confronted by the term "catastrophic risk": floods, wildfires, earthquakes, volcanic eruptions, war, terrorism, and the more human-scaled tragedies of falling bridges, derailed trains, burning buildings, or airplane crashes. But in 2009, as in 1929, the world became acutely aware that risk and chance can destroy the world of finance as they can any complicated structure built on mistaken expert understandings of how things work. Unpredicted as little as a few weeks before the meltdown on Wall Street, the economic crisis that began in 2008 exhibited the expanded scale, cross-jurisdictional reach, and resulting unmanageability of risks in a highly networked world society. A global breakdown in the financial system portended catastrophe for many nations in terms of lost jobs, homelessness, rising social unrest, increased disease incidence, and other indicators of distress. Yet, as the case of Iceland, an early victim of the meltdown, dramatically demonstrated, many sovereign states are powerless to fix problems whose causes and consequences are distributed in often non-transparent ways among agents lying partly or wholly outside national control. In addition to the well-known democratic deficits of our expert-ruled societies, these globally dispersed hazards point, as Andrew Lakoff's introduction suggests, to serious deficits in the existing institutions of risk governance.

Below, I reflect on the normative dimensions of such problems. How, with what instruments, by whom, and for whose benefit should risks, especially the incalculable ones, be governed? Four sets of difficulties have proved intransigent. First, there is the barrier of culture: how can we assess the likely impacts of events of potentially global consequence with analytic imaginations bounded by culturally conditioned ideas of rationality and by particular ways of seeing and knowing risk? Second, there is the challenge of bureaucratic reductionism: how can administrative institutions draw appropriate lessons from the past, given their tendency to simplify for convenience the richness and complexity of human experience? Third, there is the imperative of ethics: whose responsibility is it to identify who is at risk and from what or to address associated distributive questions about whose vulnerabilities are important and whose voices should count in setting priorities? Fourth, there are the constraints of economics: given the unequal impacts of risk, how should we cope with dilemmas about allocating scarce preventive and remedial resources?

I approach these problems by first reviewing how they played out, or more accurately were downplayed, in the development of quantitative risk analysis as a favored discourse of public policy. I then show how these problems manifested themselves in the two natural disasters with which this chapter began, the Asian tsunami and Hurricane Katrina. I conclude by outlining a more modest, experiential, and inclusive approach to dealing with the persistent obstacles to democratic risk governance, using analytic strategies that I term "technologies of humility."[5]

THE CALCULUS OF CONTROL

In the latter half of the terrifying twentieth century, risk became a major concern of governments. While (or possibly *because*) they had not been able to control the slides into two catastrophic world wars, advanced industrial states felt increasingly compelled to provide reassurance that they would manage their citizens' destinies better in the future. In part, this meant that states had to rein in the technologies their wars had done so much to promote: they had to show that chemicals, biological agents and (later) genetic modification of living things, transportation, nuclear weapons, and instruments of surveillance and mass communication could all be safely redeployed in the service of peace, prosperity, and welfare. In part, it meant demonstrating that public officials can foresee, and keep from materializing, new dangers on the horizon, dangers stemming from either the natural or the social world or from their unpredictable interaction. The list of such hazards seems limitless. The decades on either side of the millennium divide placed on the agenda of global risk prevention new environmental issues, such as deforestation, ozone depletion, species loss, and climate change; new threats to peace from nuclear first strikes or, after September 11, 2001, global terror; new fears of pandemics, from AIDS to avian influenza; new, seemingly ineradicable social "diseases," such as poverty, scarcity, and violations of human rights; and new economic threats from massive breakdowns in the banking and investment sectors.

Demonstrations of the state's ability to manage risks, moreover, had to be made under changing sociopolitical circumstances that challenged the legitimacy of public reason. With increasing wealth, more was at stake in getting things wrong, and the enormous successes of modern technology bred rising expectations about what could be controlled and should not be left to chance. Demands for transparency grew as publics asked to look behind the decisions of both elected and appointed rulers and questioned their expert justifications. In democratic societies, citizens gained progressively more access to information, and through the expanding power of the media and the exponential growth of nongovernmental organizations (NGOs), they also became better equipped to hold state authorities accountable for errors of omission and commission. NGOs acquired and skillfully deployed their own specialized knowledge, challenging the hegemony of government and corporate experts. At the same time, the indeterminacy and complexity of many novel risks, and their refusal to stay within neatly drawn geopolitical lines, taxed the power of nation-states to offer to global publics credible predictions and convincing remedies.

The vast and growing literature on risk chronicles the profound resulting transformations in the complexion of social and political life. To begin with, risk has shifted its locus almost imperceptibly from being principally a managerial problem to one that is seen also as deeply political; in other words, the bureaucratic task of risk management is now seen to be just one aspect of the broader enterprise of risk governance. Risk management was traditionally considered a domain for experts. Risk governance by contrast requires the involvement of citizens and their political representatives. Whereas management entailed mainly the tasks of identifying and controlling risks, often associated with single causes, governance takes as its purview the sociopolitical environments in which risks originate and concerns itself with explicitly political choices: for example, how to weigh trade-offs among competing risks, how to communicate with affected (and disaffected) publics, and how to integrate demands for social justice into analytic processes once seen as largely technical.

Many incremental changes converged to bring about this shift, changes in domains of knowledge as well as of social organization and behavior. On the side of knowledge, a key development was the emergence and spread of new formal techniques of risk analysis—aimed at disciplining the incalculable through sophisticated forms of calculation. Once the preserve of actuaries and insurers, risk assessment became by the end of the twentieth century an indispensable instrument in the toolkit of public administration. Mathematical models generating estimates of probable harm were developed for issues as diverse as tracking the dispersal of chemicals in the environment and their effects on people or ecosystems, tracing the spread of introduced genes from one organism to another, measuring the likelihood of accidents at nuclear and chemical plants, and calculating the effects of global mean temperature rise on pathogens or storm surges. The proliferation of these methods raised new questions for governments: whose knowledge should states rely on; how should they certify policy-relevant knowledge as reliable; how should expert judgments be made publicly accountable; and how should conflicts among experts, interest groups, and indeed national governments be resolved?[6]

On the side of social transformation, theorists focused, in the first instance, on the disruptive effects of risk on preexisting structures and practices. Social analysts often took the fact of risk for granted; for them, it was the distribution and consequences of risk in society, and the disturbing implications of risk for human autonomy and solidarity, that required investigation or explanation. In one famous treatment of the subject, the German sociologist Ulrich Beck sweepingly proclaimed that risk had displaced class and other economic and social variables as the primary organizing force in modern life.[7] The "risk society" Beck described seemed no longer able to rely unproblematically on science, the cornerstone of reason in public life since the Enlightenment. Through a process he termed "reflexive modernization," Beck argued, science not only provides persuasive support for the detection and assessment of risks but, because of its universal uptake, also supplies resources for skepticism and critique that prevent the construction of stable rationalities to support risk reduction. Others called attention to the relations of inequality that inevitably accompany the creation and dispersal of technological hazards and their disproportionate impacts on the economically marginal and socially disempowered.[8] Still others explored the troubling implications for democracy as risk discourse and practice came to be dominated by cadres of experts, allied with public and corporate policymakers, in the new, opaque formations of the regulatory state.[9]

By contrast, defenders of modernization and of its scientific and technological drivers downplayed the imperfections of both calculation and democracy and constructed their own implicit models of what is wrong in contemporary risk societies. Alvin Weinberg, the influential director of America's Oak Ridge National Laboratory, sounded an early alarm with his much-cited observation that policymakers were turning to scientists for answers to essentially unanswerable questions, thereby defining a potentially ungovernable domain of "trans-science."[10] But, aided by burgeoning databases and growing computer power, the technocratic advocates of risk governance rapidly regained confidence in the possibility of accurate prediction and control, even for seemingly incalculable, catastrophic risks. Accordingly, innovation could proceed unhindered, publics be reassured that someone was in charge, and limited resources be deployed to good effect if hazards escaped the managers' control. Most risks worth worrying about, the technocratic perspective holds, can be estimated on the basis of solid data, good models, and (in a new mantra for decisionmakers) "sound science." Likewise, the credibility of risk assessments can be guaranteed through the careful separation of science from politics and through impartial peer review.[11] From the technocratic standpoint, the dominant problems are to find the right experts and produce the best knowledge. Qualified experts should be able to produce meaningful hierarchies of risk and make sure that the most significant ones receive the most attention.[12]

Deviations between expert and public perceptions of risk now surfaced as a source of perplexity and alarm. Why do publics often respond negatively to risks that experts deem negligible? In looking for answers, expertise in risk analysis became coupled with tacit theories of public opinion formation. If publics worry unduly about small risks, many concluded, it must be because of superstition, media hype, technical illiteracy, poor understanding of science, or manipulation by political interests.[13] The study of public risk perception itself emerged as a new social science. Probing into the systematic variances between lay and expert assessments of relative risks, social psychologists identified several characteristics of risk that seem to enhance people's perceptions of danger: for example, novelty, non-voluntariness, and lack of control.[14] By century's end, these studies were aligned with a turn toward finding the factors that cause people to deviate from strict probability judgments in forming their reactions to risks. Broadly clustered under the heading "biases and heuristics," and building on pioneering work on prospect theory by Amos Tversky and Nobel laureate Daniel Kahneman,[15] these experimental studies characterized people's anti-probabilistic intuitions as deviations from perfect rationality induced by such habits of bad reasoning as overvaluing recent experience, paying greater heed to the probability of losses than gains, and favoring the status quo over even beneficial change.

Such research leaves intact the technocratic promise of being able to estimate risks with reasonable certainty and attributes the discrepancies between expert judgments and public perceptions to laypeople's built-in (and, by definition, distorting) cognitive biases. Concern about risks, especially those deemed small or negligible by experts, is routinely, and asymmetrically, labeled as biased or irrational and treated as needing special cognitive explanation. This stance reinforces the power divide between publics and experts, and by denigrating the rational decision-making potential of the demos, it implicitly justifies anti-democratic policymaking in the public's own best interests.[16] It presumes that risk policy should not concern itself with distorting contextual variables that impermissibly alter "perception" but should look only at mathematically calculated probabilities of harm — the sole reasonable basis for setting policy priorities and allocating funds. Rationality, for the expert assessors of risk, remains squarely on the side of scientific prediction and management.

Organizational sociology has made some inroads into this binary framework of reason and unreason. This literature displays the embeddedness of hazardous technological artifacts and risky human behaviors in organizational routines and practices that cannot be separated from the physical or biological pathways through which hazards arise.[17] It is virtually a truism that human factors can contribute as much to risk creation as the inanimate features of functioning technologies. Accident investigations frequently ascribe the fault to a system's human implementation, through concepts such as operator or human error. Hence, ideas like Charles Perrow's "tight coupling"[18] of complex technological systems or Diane Vaughan's "normalization of deviance"[19] are now seen as integral to the design of safe technological infrastructures. Yet the persistent notion that the causes of failure can be separately attributed to human factors, especially the mistakes of individuals, exonerates the system's designers. It perpetuates the dream of perfect technological systems that would be fail-safe if only their human components performed as flawlessly as their non-human parts. The human element of risky environments becomes, in this way of reckoning, simply another "factor" to be incorporated into the framework of rational calculation and design.

None of this offers much comfort to proponents of democratic risk governance in a world undergoing rapid social, technological, and environmental integration and change. Such governance would foster discovery and innovation in a world in which, all concede, zero risk is an unattainable ideal, but it would also take into account public preferences and concerns, as well as cross-cultural differences in needs and wants. The risk society discerned by Beck and others, however, offers few compass points by which to steer developments in science and technology in beneficial directions or to choose between alternative pathways, each entailing some risks. It comes too close to legitimating all forms of risk aversiveness. In that sense, it is not a satisfying answer to the demands of what sociologists have begun to call "knowledge societies": societies in which knowledge is the new form of capital and its effective production and use are essential for securing human welfare.

Still less promising are the analyses of risk experts who leave unexamined the very notions of "risk" and "expertise," who attribute failures of risk management mainly to human error, and who blame public fear and anxiety on laypeople's ignorance and incompetence in technical matters. Even organizational sociology's valiant efforts to restore the human to the domain of technical analysis have done little to draw attention to the political challenges of risk governance. As noted, a superficial reading of this literature can reinforce the belief in the perfectibility of machines that has proved such an impediment to accommodating wide-ranging social concerns about the production and management of risk.

Can we, then, imagine a regime of democratic risk governance that allows for the possibility of change and yet makes room for the reasonable questions, doubts, fears, and preferences of non-expert publics? Before attempting answers, let us first look more closely at the two events that opened this chapter—the tsunami and the hurricane—focusing not only on the foreseeability of the events themselves but also on the particular ways in which each one's consequences played out in the affected societies.

UNNATURAL DISASTERS

On the day after Christmas 2004, a massive earthquake measuring over 9.0 on the Richter scale occurred in the Indian Ocean, with its epicenter off the northern tip of the Indonesian island of Sumatra. The violent, minutes-long shaking produced a vast tidal wave, or tsunami, that radiated out as far as Kenya and Somalia on the eastern coast of Africa. It left more than 220,000 dead, and many times that number bereft of shelter and livelihood, in Indonesia, Sri Lanka, India, Thailand, and several other countries. The tragedy elicited an unprecedented global humanitarian response, though unequal it seems to the full dimensions of the tragedy.[20] While the scale of the relief effort generated its own tensions and controversies (was relief going to the right people, was it being used for the right purposes?), a second debate crystallized around the issue of preparedness. Why did so many die? Why were they not better forewarned?

Following the disaster, many commentators remarked that the Indian Ocean has no tsunami detection system of the kind that has existed for the Pacific Rim since 1949. Based in Hawaii, the Pacific Tsunami Warning Center uses seismic and oceanographic data to calculate the threat of a tidal wave following an earthquake and sends out warnings to regions likely to be affected. Analysts also noted, however, that such warnings could only be effective if they were communicated in timely fashion to the populations at risk and if the recipients were equipped to take preventive action on the basis of the warnings they received. In fact, tsunamis are relatively rare in the Indian Ocean, and human response capacities were correspondingly undeveloped. For example, in some places people did not recognize the warning sign of the sea retreating from the shore before it returned with killer force. Their curiosity aroused, both children and adults walked out to look at the fish left stranded on the shore, with fatal results. Communication broke down between and even within countries. Though several hours passed between the earthquake in Indonesia and the waves reaching India and Sri Lanka, people in those more distant countries were still not warned.

Although the waves took the lives of both rich and poor, loss and destruction were not evenly distributed. In the hardest-hit fishing communities, women and children died in larger numbers than men, who were physically better able to survive or remained relatively safe far out at sea. According to an Oxfam report produced three months after the event, three to four times as many women died as men in surveyed regions in Indonesia, Sri Lanka, and India.[21] Aid to the survivors also divided to some extent along social and economic lines. Up to two thousand European tourists, many holidaying in exclusive Thai resorts, lost their lives. A tiny fraction of the total death toll, they nonetheless received the greatest share of media and medical attention in the disaster's immediate aftermath, contributing to a somewhat artificial sense of the disaster's global reach. Tourists' families benefited from the first efforts to identify the missing and the dead through DNA tests.[22] And allegations grew and persisted that relief efforts helped the rich more than the poor.[23] Untouchables in India complained that they were among the slowest to receive aid.

The second disaster struck the United States, at the opposite pole of wealth and power from the countries hit by the Asian tsunami. On August 29, 2005, Hurricane Katrina made landfall near New Orleans in Louisiana, a city celebrated for its distinctive multicultural heritage, architecture, food, and creative traditions. Built largely below sea level, New Orleans has relied on a system of levees to protect itself from flooding, but these were designed for at most a Category 4 hurricane and were overwhelmed as Katrina reached Category 5 strength in its rush from Florida to Louisiana. Instead of merely overflowing the barriers, floodwaters breached the levees, causing breaks as much as two hundred feet in length, with severe consequences for the city. Water from Lake Pontchartrain, in particular, poured through the breached 17th Street and Canal Street levee into the heart of the city. Before and after photographs showed block after flooded block of downtown New Orleans with sheets of water where previously there had been neatly gridded streets with houses in between.

Unlike the tsunami, which caught most of its victims completely unawares, Katrina came with prior warnings, beginning as much as three days before. Indeed, the National Weather Service predicted the possible breakdown of the levees, and Mayor Ray Nagin ordered a mandatory evacuation of the city on August 28, a day before the hurricane struck. Not everyone, however, was in a position to heed the order, and once again the disaster's worst effects were felt most viscerally by the economically and socially marginal: the poor, the sick, the old, and the infirm. Poignant stories included the deaths of hospitalized patients deprived of electrical life-support systems, residents of old-age homes, and people unable to escape from houses that were too low to offer refuge from rapidly rising floodwaters.

The disaster was one of the worst in recorded American history. It left some 1200 people dead, devastated a culturally vibrant city, and entailed by September 2005 an estimated $35 billion in damage claims for the insurance industry, far surpassing the inflation-adjusted damage claims of $20 billion arising from Hurricane Andrew in 1992.[24] New Orleans, in Katrina's wake, looked and smelled according to one account like a landfill, blanketed in twenty-two million tons of debris, besides the more than a million appliances, thousands of abandoned cars, and toxic materials from household chemicals to more hazardous substances like mercury.[25] More than a quarter of the city's housing stock, up to 50,000 houses by official estimates, was so badly damaged that it seemed impossible to salvage. In a city where nearly a fourth of the residents lived below the poverty line, it was unclear how many homeowners would have the resources to bear the massive cost of reconstruction.[26]

The political mess the disaster left was equally monumental. There were, to begin with, charges and countercharges between a Republican national government and Democratic state and local authorities about blame for failures of warning and, even more, of emergency response. An immediate target was Michael D. Brown, head of the Federal Emergency Management Agency (FEMA), whose lack of competence in disaster relief was widely cited as evidence of unacceptable cronyism in the Bush administration. Brown's public comments blaming the victims for some of their own troubles helped neither his nor his agency's image. On a visit to the Houston Astrodome, where thousands of destitute New Orleans refugees had taken shelter, the president's mother, Barbara Bush, compounded the appearance of callousness by saying, "And so many of the people in the arena here, you know, were underprivileged anyway, so this is working very well for them."[27] In his two-year retrospective on Katrina, Michael Grunwald, a reporter for *Time* magazine, shunted the blame further back in history, to the Army Corps of Engineers, whose "teach Mother Nature a lesson" philosophy, he wrote, had destroyed the city's natural storm barriers and created the preconditions for disaster.[28] An early adherent of project-specific cost-benefit analysis, the Corps represents to many the very model of a self-described rational agency—whose calculations papered over the fact that its projects grew out of the most blatant congressional earmarks and pork-barrel politics.[29]

Geographically and culturally separated, the two disasters present some striking parallels. In each case, advanced technologies of prediction were actually or theoretically available but were either not accessible or else incapable of getting vulnerable people to take precautionary action. In each, how people behaved before and, above all, during and after the catastrophic event influenced the extent and distribution of damages. In each, too, the disaster affected the more and less endowed—the rich and the poor, the old and the young, men and women—in dramatically different ways. On the whole, people with more resources were better able to fend for themselves, both when warnings were delivered and after disaster struck. The losses in each case reflected not only the physically destructive impacts of earthquake, wind, and water but also the unexpected entwining of these forces with features of human behavior, technological capacity, and social organization. In this sense the disasters, seen in hindsight, seem anything but "natural."

Following events of tragic magnitude, it is common to ask whether, if the same thing happened again, we would be better prepared. That is the salient question policymakers have confronted in both the tsunami-devastated regions of Asia and the hurricane-torn city of New Orleans. Indeed, just two weeks after Hurricane Katrina, I myself was asked whether I would advise the construction of higher levees in New Orleans. After all, my interlocutor added, isn't this the sort of question that a scholar of risk from a leading university should be prepared to answer? What use is all that scholarship if it cannot inform decisionmakers confronted with very practical problems of how to choose between competing options? Should a tsunami detection system be installed in the Indian Ocean; should a drowned city be rebuilt on its old fault lines?

Decisionmakers face many such urgent questions in the aftermath of disastrous events, and it is important for them to make choices that are both responsive to sufferers' immediate needs and capable of minimizing future loss. In just over twenty years, profoundly difficult issues, technical as well as political, confronted decisionmakers in India after the Bhopal gas leak; the former Soviet Union after the Chernobyl explosion; Britain after the BSE (bovine spongiform encephalopathy), or "mad cow," epidemic; New York City after the 9/11 terrorist attacks; Toronto after the outbreak of SARS (severe acute respiratory syndrome); Indonesia after the tsunami; and New Orleans after Hurricane Katrina. One should not minimize the case-specific challenges of deciding how to clean up, offer treatment, make whole, restore safety and trust, and rebuild community and confidence after such cataclysmic risk-into-reality episodes.

And yet, the foregoing list, which could be indefinitely expanded, is instructive about the limits of professional assessments. Globally, there is no society that is not today a risk society. But risks of all kinds become apparent throughout the contemporary world only after they have materialized into harms. Given the range and severity of injurious events that can overtake us unawares and the woeful shortcomings of emergency response despite decades of expert risk management, even in wealthy nations, the important question is not only how to predict events more accurately but how to ensure greater resilience if and when they occur. It is to ask how institutional and social capacities can be cultivated so as to ensure that bad events, when they inevitably happen, do less damage to solidarity and human lives.[30]

Former president Bill Clinton, writing six months after the tsunami as the United Nations special envoy for tsunami relief, noted the need to involve those at the bottom of the opportunity ladder in such remedial processes:

> Finally, we must do all we can to assure that the voices of the most vulnerable are heard. Will women survivors be involved in the design and execution of the recovery process? Will their property rights be protected? Will the Dalits (also known as the "untouchables") of India be discriminated against? Will poor families get documentation for their assets and have access to lines of credit? Will national governments give localities greater flexibility to meet their particular needs? Will children who survived be able to get back to school? Will the disaster usher in a new chapter in the peace processes in Sri Lanka and Aceh, thereby making it easier for aid to be distributed and reconstruction to take place wherever it's needed?[31]

The broader challenge for risk governance, as Clinton, the consummate politician, implicitly recognized, is to move away from a near-exclusive focus on causes and probabilities—on calculating the incalculable—toward a deeper understanding of the contexts within which injuries are experienced, and often exacerbated, with painful inequity. It is to end the downward spiral of expert rationality denigrating the wisdom of the multitude and the values of democracy and to promote instead an upward spiral of inclusion that builds on people's legitimate expectations of equality, representation, fairness, and public accountability.

TECHNOLOGIES OF HUMILITY

The standard definition of risk used by policymakers worldwide is that it is the probability of harm times the magnitude of harm. This colorless, quantitative definition performs two functions, both of which are necessary from the standpoint of maintaining official credibility. First, it helps to naturalize risk—that is, to place it "out there" in the real world, as a feature of that world's natural functioning. From this definition it is easy to draw the implication that "zero risk" is an unattainable state; harms will occur, it is only natural, and the important thing for policymakers to know is the likely frequency of any particular harm and how grievously it will affect those it strikes.

Second, the traditional definition provides a blueprint for what decisionmakers need to measure in order to assess risks responsibly. In its widely circulated 1983 report on risk assessment, the U.S. National Research Council laid out a sequence of steps that together comprise risk analysis: hazard identification, exposure assessment, risk characterization, risk communication, risk management.[32] Each step can be broken down into further subtasks that operationalize it; indeed, each has become a node around which new analytic techniques and new forms of expertise have crystallized over time.

Thus, highly technical methods of hazard identification, exposure assessment, and risk characterization have developed with respect to specific categories of risk. For example, today there are entire communities of experts dedicated to studying the environmental dispersal and human health effects of single pollutants like radiation, mercury, dioxin, and small airborne particulates. Tsunamis and hurricanes along with many other natural hazards, such as volcanic eruptions, climate change, deforestation, and biodiversity loss, have all given rise to bodies of expert knowledge produced by global networks of scientists. High-risk technologies, such as chemical or nuclear plants and air traffic control, command their own specialist risk analysts. Since the threat of global terrorism emerged on the public agenda, it too has begun to generate new forms of expertise — for instance, the capacity to detect suspicious movements in crowds by means of computer models or trained human eyes. Few large regulatory bureaucracies could think of functioning without their in-house experts in risk-benefit analysis and, increasingly, risk communication.

The work of such experts is, of course, invaluable for decision-makers charged with protecting publics from risk. Accumulated expert knowledge represents an important kind of learning from the past — in this case, through science's powerful methods of gathering data and building on its own prior successes. But as the tsunami and hurricane cases show, there is no necessary correlation between the scientific understanding of a particular risky phenomenon or system and the devastation experienced when the risk it presents mutates into reality. All our knowledge of tsunamis and hurricanes could not prevent stupendous damage in Sumatra and Louisiana or even ensure prompt and effective assistance to those left stranded in each event's wake. Nor are these examples *sui generis*. In cases like Bhopal, BSE, Chernobyl, or 9/11, expert knowledge of many relevant subsystems failed to produce the synthesizing forecasts that might have helped guard against those particular events. Despite all efforts at calculation, these realized risks arose in contexts in which the harms were, for all practical purposes, incalculable in advance. If they could not have been calculated, we may ask, could they nevertheless have been mitigated through improved governance?

That question requires us to turn on its head the analytic perspective so carefully nurtured through decades of effort to predict and control risks. For where management implies a top-down perspective, that of the manager in charge of a system, governance in democratic societies necessarily works from the bottom up — through the delegation of responsibility to rulers who are trusted to exercise power legitimately, on behalf of the people. The predictive stance relies on the manager's presumptively superior knowledge and expertise. Governance, by contrast, draws its strength from below, by aggregating communal knowledge and experience, preferences and concerns that no science has brought under its control. Not coincidentally, politics is often called "the art of the possible," a quotation attributed to Otto von Bismarck, one of the architects of the modern welfare state; it is not the science of the probable. Humility, not hubris, is the animating spirit of governance. History, not futurology, is its richest resource.

Recognizing the flaws and failures of traditional risk management does not mean that one has to abandon analysis. Governance, too, can rest upon its own approaches to systematic, analytic thought. Indeed, as I have suggested elsewhere,[33] it is possible to abstract from the case-study literature on disasters, as well as from critical studies of risk analysis and policy-relevant science, four focal points for the "technologies of humility" that can inform risk governance. These are framing, vulnerability, distribution, and deliberative learning. Together, they address the questions that must be asked in seeking solutions to governance problems in any risky environment: What do we know about the risk and how do we know it? Who is likely to be hurt? How will losses be distributed? And how can we reflect most effectively on our collective experiences of vulnerability and loss?

FRAMING

Policy scholars have recognized for some time that the quality of the solution to a perceived social problem depends on the adequacy of its original framing.[34] If a problem is framed too narrowly, too broadly, or simply in the wrong terms, the solution will suffer from the same defects. Was the primary problem in New Orleans that the levees were designed for hurricanes of lesser force than Katrina or that building large parts of a city below sea level was intrinsically a recipe for disaster? Along with hurricane prediction, did anyone conduct a citywide vulnerability study to see which individuals and neighborhoods would likely suffer most? Did the focus on hurricane prediction distract people's attention from the massive emergency relief efforts that would be required if the levees broke? Was the tsunami a failure of technology or of social systems (or both)? Will it help to install an advanced tsunami detection system in the Indian Ocean, or will the warnings generated by such a system fail to travel (as happened with the news of the 2004 tsunami) or to influence affected people's behavior (as happened with the warnings around Katrina)? Few policy cultures have adopted systematic methods for asking such questions about the dominant framings of risk, despite high-profile calls for doing so.[35] Frame analysis accordingly remains a well-recognized, critically important, but surprisingly neglected branch of policymaking.

VULNERABILITY

Risk analysts have traditionally viewed at-risk individuals or populations as passive objects in the path of the risk to be characterized. People are seen as exposed to the risks that the manager wishes to control; their exposure is then assessed through techniques of formal quantification. One problem with this approach is that the risk manager's judgment is taken as the reference point for determining vulnerability rather than the affected subjects' self-perceptions, let alone their historical experience. Yet how people perceive their own vulnerability may be radically different in meaning and intensity from the perceptions of outsiders. As Barbara Bush's unthinking comment about "underprivileged" New Orleans residents showed, outsiders may have believed that those communities had a lot less to lose than did members of the communities themselves; culture and cohesion do not typically figure in risk assessors' estimates of costs and benefits. By contrast, it probably did not take a tidal wave to show the fishing families of the Indian Ocean region how precarious were their livelihoods and means of subsistence — or how completely their futures were tied to nature's fury or beneficence.

A second, related problem is that risk assessment tends to overlook the social foundations of vulnerability and to classify at-risk populations in accordance with supposedly objective physical and biological criteria.[36] In the effort to produce policy-relevant assessments, human populations are often classified into groups that are thought to be differently affected by the hazard in question (for example, most susceptible, maximally exposed, genetically predisposed, children, or women). These approaches not only disregard potentially salient differences within groups but conceptualize individuals in statistical terms, as members of aggregates. This characterization leaves out of the emerging calculus of vulnerability factors such as history, place, and social connectedness that may, in fact, play crucial roles in determining the resilience of human societies. As stories from the tsunami-affected regions showed, groups deemed similar on the basis of objectively measurable criteria coped very differently with disaster because of divergences in the strengths of their communal knowledges and networks.[37]

Through participation in the analysis of vulnerability—and its mirror image, resilience—ordinary citizens may be able to correct some of these defects.[38] They would in any event regain their status as active subjects in risk governance rather than remain the impersonal objects of yet another distanced expert calculation.

DISTRIBUTION

Perhaps the most striking similarity between the tsunami and the hurricane was that both disproportionately afflicted the poor. So notable were the socioeconomic disparities in New Orleans that David Ellwood, dean of Harvard University's John F. Kennedy School of Government, said, "It took a terrible hurricane, but the poor in America, who have languished largely unmentioned by politicians of both parties, are visible once again."[39] Arguably, as the Oxfam analysis of discrepant gender-based impacts suggests, the tsunami played a comparable role in making visible the inequalities between women and men that were always there for any discerning observer to see. Such distributive effects, however, are not part of the agenda of classical risk analysis. To be sure, a law or policy may specify that the distribution of risk for different social groups needs to be taken into account, as under the 1994 Clinton-era U.S. policy for considering the environmental justice implications of governmental programs and actions. But in the absence of such mandates, mapping inequality is not within the normal technical repertoire of exposure assessment.

In a regime of risk governance, by contrast, inequality would always be on the agenda because it is a factor that immediately and obviously affects people's responses to harmful occurrences. Distributive issues would simply be part of the context that decisionmakers are responsible for understanding in their efforts to protect those most at risk. In deliberative settings, inequality would be flagged by those for whom risk policy is supposed to be made, much as claimants for environmental justice in an earlier era signaled their needs to regulators who had ignored the tendency of risks to cluster in poor and socially marginal communities. In a world where the task of dealing with risk focuses on contexts as well as causes and takes into account subjective experience as well as objective measurement, it would not take a hurricane to make visible the plight of the poor.

The capacity to learn is constrained, as I have suggested, by the limiting features of the frame within which institutions reflect on their prior actions. Institutions see only what their governing discourses and practices allow them to see. Thus the framework of risk assessment continually reorients the expert learner's attention back toward prediction, with its emphasis on improved quantitative modeling, its insistence on probabilistic thinking, and its primary orientation toward the management of causes. It is hardly surprising, then, that technological fixes hold such high appeal for policy professionals or that so much of the immediate post-disaster discourse in our two cases focused on whether to build an Indian Ocean tsunami detection system or to raise higher the levees in New Orleans.

Experience, however, tells different stories to different people. It changes with the angle of observation. Even when the outward facts of a tragedy are more or less unambiguous (as they often are not)—what happened, who died, how many were hurt—its causes and consequences may still be open to many different readings. Just as there can be no single explanation for what caused the great wars of the last century, so major disasters cannot be attributed to unitary causes that lead in turn to inadequate patchwork remedies. The current design of most risk management institutions promotes the accumulation of expert knowledge and the revision of policy without challenging the manager's framing assumptions. In the shift toward risk governance, the aim should be to construct institutions of civic deliberation through which societies can actively reflect on ambiguity and assess the strengths and weaknesses of alternative explanations. Deliberative learning, in this sense, may be more messy in its processes and more modest in its expectations than expert practices of calculating risk, but it would be rightfully more ambitious in seeking to learn from the full extent of relevant experience and in building, on that basis, more resilient societies.

Contrasts between the managerial and participatory approaches can be found in the project reports of two major development agencies, the Asian Development Bank (ADB) and the United States Agency for International Development (USAID), neither known for especially nimble adjustments to human experience. In its summary of the tsunami impacts in India, ADP describes the situation in the quantitative and systemic discourses typical of international lending institutions. Impacts are represented in aggregate numbers (casualties, affected areas, economic damage). ADB's responses too are impersonal and system-wide: restoration of livelihoods, rehabilitation of damaged infrastructure, and capacity-building among disaster management professionals.[40] USAID's self-presentation, by contrast, focuses on "rebuilding lives," and its Indian story is one about democracy in an unlikely place. In tsunami-affected Cuddalore, near the Tamil Nadu capital of Chennai, USAID spotlights a children's parliament that participated in reallocating government relief aid to schools in the region. Working in conjunction with local initiatives, USAID states that the parliament "has provided trauma counseling and back-to-school initiatives, as well as children's libraries, parks, puppet shows, and street plays." Its most recent programs "center on psychosocial care, health and hygiene, and children's rights."[41] Some of this language may well be development jargon, and yet the approaches of the two institutions seem to capture some of the differences between the calculative and democratic impulses and the differences they may entail in the forms and targets of post-disaster aid.

CONCLUSION

Humanity's attempt to grapple with risk in the twentieth century turned out to be a protean task. The concept at the center of attention — risk itself — proved to be as varied in its causes as nature itself and as inevitable in its tragic consequences as the sufferings of the poor and the powerless. From early roots in accident and fire prevention and in natural hazard management, risk grew to be a central preoccupation of public authorities seeking to justify their existence, a concern for experts evaluating novel technological promises, and an organizing concept for social theorists. No one in today's networked world can fail to feel at risk from some, perhaps many, causes. Much of the work of regulation and large segments of private corporate enterprise are directed toward controlling risk in one form or another, whether in health care, hazardous industries, environmental protection, computer security, anti-terror activities, or financial systems management.

Paradoxically, in what could perhaps be seen as a specific working out of Ulrich Beck's notion of reflexive modernization, the spread of risk in contemporary societies has undermined the very property that gave the notion its original power: namely, its amenability to calculation. Risk is the product of human imaginations bent on the taming of chance. Yet as modern humanity became more and more averse to leaving any aspect of its fate to be ruled entirely by chance, risk spilled out of the envelopes of measurement and prediction and became incalculable. In this process, I have suggested, risk also escaped the control of expert managers and became a problem for democratic politics: risk management, more particularly, gave way to the broader challenges of risk governance.

This fundamental shift requires a rethinking of the conceptual tools and analytic strategies with which human societies seek to cope with risk. Unlike management, governance cannot be conceived as a top-down process largely the preserve of technocrats trained in specialized practices of prediction and control. Rather, like any political undertaking, democratic risk governance demands constant engagement with its authorizing public constituencies. It calls for a comprehensive mining of collective experience geared toward building resilience rather than providing issue-specific prevention or relief. It also requires new approaches to analysis—technologies of humility as I have called them—using methods that look backward on the past, with due respect for the multiplicity and ambiguity of human experience.

From historical experiences of risk in the real world, including the Asian tsunami and Hurricane Katrina, four analytic focal points have emerged as salient for risk governance: framing, vulnerability, distribution, and deliberative learning. These draw attention to the social and political environments in which risk morphs into reality, and they shift the weight of analysis from causes to contexts. They not only reorganize thought in new ways but hold out the promise of wider public engagement in the practices of risk analysis. In these respects, technologies of humility may provide a bridge to a post-Enlightenment politics that is not afraid to confront its unruly past or its incalculable future.

NOTES

1 See, for instance, the argument that genetic explanations artificially narrow the problems of biological development in Richard Lewontin, *The Triple Helix: Gene, Organism, and Environment* (Cambridge, MA: Harvard University Press, 2000).

2 Ian Hacking, *The Taming of Chance* (Cambridge: Cambridge University Press, 1990). See also Theodore M. Porter, *The Rise of Statistical Thinking, 1820–1900* (Princeton, NJ: Princeton University Press, 1986).

3 U.S. Department of Energy, *The Manhattan Project: An Interactive History*, http://www.mbe.doe.gov/me70/manhattan/trinity.htm.

4 In an eerie replay, the activation of the Large Hadron Collider in Geneva in 2008 ignited a similar debate over the potentially catastrophic effects of an experiment in high-energy physics.

5 For an earlier exposition of this concept, see Sheila Jasanoff, "Technologies of Humility: Citizen Participation in Governing Science," *Minerva* 41, no. 3 (2003): 223–44.

6 On the role of expert advisory committees in dealing with some of these issues, see Sheila Jasanoff, *The Fifth Branch: Science Advisers as Policymakers* (Cambridge, MA: Harvard University Press, 1990). On differences in national approaches to assessing and managing risk, see Ronald Brickman, Sheila Jasanoff, and Thomas Ilgen, *Controlling Chemicals: The Politics of Regulation in Europe and the United States* (Ithaca, NY: Cornell University Press, 1985); and Sheila Jasanoff, *Designs on Nature: Science and Democracy in Europe and the United States* (Princeton, NJ: Princeton University Press, 2005).

7 Ulrich Beck, *Risk Society: Towards a New Modernity* (London: Sage Publications, 1992).

8 See, for example, David Harvey, "The Environment of Justice," in *Living with Nature: Environmental Politics as Cultural Discourse*, ed. Frank Fischer and Maarten A. Hajer (Oxford: Oxford University Press, 1999), 153–60.

9 Langdon Winner, "On Not Hitting the Tar-Baby," in *The Whale and the Reactor: A Search for Limits in an Age of High Technology* (Chicago: University of Chicago Press, 1986), chap. 8. Also see Sheila Jasanoff, "Civilization and Madness: The Great BSE Scare of 1996," *Public Understanding of Science* 6 (July 1997): 221–32.

10 Alvin M. Weinberg, "Science and Trans-Science," *Minerva* 10, no. 2 (1972): 209–22.

11 The most authoritative exposition of these views for policy purposes was a report of the U.S. National Research Council. That report laid out the classic risk assessment–risk management paradigm, which holds that the scientific task of assessing risk should be separated as far as possible from the social and political tasks of

managing risk. See U.S. National Research Council (NRC), *Risk Assessment in the Federal Government: Managing the Process* (Washington, DC: National Academies Press, 1983).

12 For an elaboration of this position, see John D. Graham and Jonathan Baert Wiener, eds., *Risk vs. Risk: Tradeoffs in Protecting Health and the Environment* (Cambridge, MA: Harvard University Press, 1995).

13 Influential articulations of these views include Cass R. Sunstein, *Risk and Reason: Safety, Law, and the Environment* (Cambridge: Cambridge University Press, 2002); and Stephen Breyer, Breaking the Vicious Circle: Toward Effective Risk Regulation (Cambridge, MA: Harvard University Press, 1993).

14 See, for example, Paul Slovic, Baruch Fischhoff, and Sarah Lichtenstein, "Facts Versus Fears: Understanding Perceived Risk," in *Judgment under Uncertainty: Heuristics and Biases*, ed. Daniel Kahneman, Paul Slovic, and Amos Tversky (New York: Cambridge University Press, 1982), 463–89.

15 Daniel Kahneman and Amos Tversky, "Prospect Theory: An Analysis of Decision under Risk," *Econometrica* 47, no. 2 (1979): 263–92.

16 See, for example, Cass R. Sunstein, *Laws of Fear: Beyond the Precautionary Principle* (New York: Cambridge University Press, 2005). Also see Cass R. Sunstein and Richard Zeckhauser, "Overreaction to Fearsome Risks," RWP08-079 (Harvard Kennedy School Faculty Research Working Paper Series, December 2008), http://web.hks.harvard.edu/publications/workingpapers/citation.aspx?PubId=6152.

17 See, for instance, Bridget Hutter and Michael Power, eds., *Organizational Encounters with Risk* (Cambridge: Cambridge University Press, 2005).

18 Charles Perrow, *Normal Accidents: Living with High Risk Technologies* (New York: Basic Books, 1984).

19 Diane Vaughan, *The Challenger Launch Decision: Risky Technology, Culture, and Deviance at NASA* (Chicago: University of Chicago Press, 1996).

20 As of September 15, 2005, Reuters Tsunami Aidwatch reported that donor governments had pledged over $7 billion and private donors some $5 billion in aid for emergency relief and reconstruction. Reuters AlertNet, "Big Tsunami Donors Allocate Three-Quarters of Funds," Reuters Tsunami Aidwatch, http://www.alertnet.org/thefacts/aidtracker/ (accessed September 2005).

21 Oxfam International, "The Tsunami's Impact on Women," (Oxfam Briefing Note, March 2005), http://www.oxfam.org/en/policy/bn050326-tsunami-women.

22 I was in Chennai, India, on the day of the disaster and remained in India for the following two weeks. I therefore had the opportunity to follow the media coverage in person while it was unfolding.

23 Oxfam International, "Poorest People Suffered the Most from the Tsunami," press release, June 25, 2005. Oxfam cited three reasons: greater vulnerability, coincidence (impact was greatest in poor regions), and focus of some relief efforts on landowners and businesses.

24 The $35 billion estimate was a consensus figure, but estimates ranged as high as $60 billion. Joseph B. Treaster, "Early Damage Estimates for Rita Much Lower than for Katrina," *New York Times*, September 24, 2005. But see also Associated Press, "Katrina Damage Estimate Hits $125B," *USA Today*, September 9, 2005.

25 Jennifer Medina, "In New Orleans, the Trashman Will Have to Move Mountains," *New York Times*, October 16, 2005.

26 Adam Nossiter, "Thousands of Demolitions Are Likely in New Orleans," *New York Times*, October 23, 2005.

27 *Daily Telegraph*, "Barbara Bush: Evacuees Doing Very Well," September 5, 2005, http://www.telegraph.co.uk/news/1497817/Barbara-Bush-evacuees-doing-very-well.html.

28 Michael Grunwald, "The Threatening Storm," *Time*, July 2, 2007.

29 On the use of cost-benefit analysis by the Army Corps of Engineers, see Theodore M. Porter, *Trust in Numbers: The Pursuit of Objectivity in Science and Public Life* (Princeton, NJ: Princeton University Press, 1995).

30 On the destruction of solidarity, see Kai Erikson, *Everything in Its Path: Destruction of Community in the Buffalo Creek Flood* (New York: Simon and Schuster, 1976).

31 William Jefferson Clinton, "Six Months After," *New York Times*, June 22, 2005.

32 NRC, Risk Assessment.

33 Jasanoff, "Technologies of Humility."

34 Donald A. Schön and Martin Rein, *Frame Reflection: Toward the Resolution of Intractable Policy Controversies* (New York: Basic Books, 1994). See also Jasanoff, *Designs on Nature*.

35 Paul C. Stern and Harvey V. Fineberg, eds., *Understanding Risk: Informing Decisions in a Democratic Society* (Washington, DC: National Academy Press, 1996).

36 For some examples, see Alan Irwin and Brian Wynne, eds., *Misunderstanding Science? The Public Reconstruction of Science and Technology* (Cambridge: Cambridge University Press, 1996).

37 One interesting puzzle was how isolated and primitive tribal groups survived on India's Andaman and Nicobar islands though many living there under more advanced socioeconomic conditions perished in the tsunami's wake. See, for instance, Neelesh Misra, "Ancient Jarawa Tribe Survives Tsunami," Associated Press, January 6, 2005.

38 Both vulnerability analysis and resilience analysis are terms of art in the analytic repertoire of climate change sciences. It is questionable how far these technical exercises have moved toward incorporating democratic ideals.

39 David T. Ellwood, "Empowering the Poor," *Boston Globe*, September 27, 2005.

40 Asian Development Bank, "India: Tsunami Summary," March 6, 2006, http://www.adb.org/media/articles/2005/6684_India_tsunami_disaster/default.asp.

41 U.S. Agency for International Development (USAID), "Making Headlines and Change: Children's Parliament in Cuddalore," *Tsunami Reconstruction*, December 2007, http://www.usaid.gov/locations/asia/documents/tsunami/tsunami_update_december_2007.pdf.

CHAPTER TWO

Private Choices, Public Harms |
The Evolution of National Disaster Organizations in the United States

PATRICK S. ROBERTS

While emergency management agencies in the United States have evolved to provide more public assistance for a greater range of disasters than ever before, several trends in American government have led to confusion about the goals of emergency preparedness and the proper role of the federal government in a complex web of management organizations. Politicization, bureaucratization, deference to states and localities, privatization, and tensions between security and non-security missions complicate efforts at preparing for the shifting category of "disaster."[1] The success the Federal Emergency Management Agency (FEMA) enjoyed in coordinating preparation and response efforts during the 1990s was the exception, not the rule. FEMA and its predecessors have always been small, coordinating agencies without the capacity to govern by command.

The diffuse, multilayered federal system of government does not provide much guidance as to who should bear the risk of disaster, whether individuals, states, localities, or the nation as a whole. Greater centralization of authority in the federal government and increased hierarchical control offers one alternative for how to prepare for future disasters.[2] Hierarchy alone, however, is a poor tool with which to prepare for disasters and emergencies.

Further privatizing government services and allowing citizens to assume greater risk as individuals offers another alternative already common in other policy areas, including health care and retirement insurance.[3] Nevertheless, a democratic majority has reached a rough consensus that preparing for disaster is a shared national responsibility. In the 2008 presidential campaign, candidates from both major parties assumed that disaster response was an issue for the president and the federal government and therefore a public responsibility. Actually governing disaster preparation and response, however, requires a networked form of government that links federal, state, and local levels of government as well as private organizations. These agencies and organizations share common goals but are not subject to direct command.

Despite modest capacity and authority, at its best a national disaster agency has been an important node for establishing agreement about the broad missions and purposes of emergency management. FEMA was best able to manage risk when it enjoyed the support of the president, key members of Congress, and networks of emergency managers at various levels of government and in the private sector. Successful disaster preparation and response occurs not through command from above—reorganizations like the creation of the Department of Homeland Security breed chaos[4]—but through loose networks of formal organizations and informal professions that maintain broad agreement about shared goals and responsibilities. The development of emergency management in the U.S. context offers important considerations for future domestic policy and for the international context, where emergency management networks are even more fluid and multilayered.

FROM CIVIL DEFENSE TO "PREPAREDNESS"

Understanding the problems faced by contemporary emergency management agencies requires exploring why emergency responsibilities were lodged in various levels of government and how over time the United States defined what constitutes an emergency. Well before the homeland security era, responsibilities for security from attack and security from natural disasters were intertwined. The first emergency preparedness agencies arose in response to fear of nuclear attack. The National Security Act of 1947 created the National Security Resources Board (NSRB).

The NSRB, along with the Office of Civil Defense Planning, was charged with providing a continuous state of readiness.[5] From the beginning, the Cold War was a national effort, as the Soviet atomic test of 1949 and the Korean War catalyzed support for a system of preparedness against nuclear attack. The media fueled a sense of vulnerability through stories about how the A-bomb could leave cities pulverized in a matter of hours.[6] Civil defense became a public and national effort, as people believed that Des Moines and Detroit, for example, not just New York City, were targets.

At the same time, managers with responsibilities beyond nuclear defense advocated a policy of "dual use," so that the same organizations, training, and equipment could be used to prepare for both deliberate attack *and* natural disasters. Proponents of civil defense supported the idea because they believed that local agencies would be more likely to engage in nuclear attack preparedness if they could also use federal plans and resources to prepare for more frequent natural disasters. In 1948, Russell Hopley, the director of the Office of Civil Defense Planning, submitted a report to secretary of defense James Forrestal that announced the creation of a comprehensive civil defense agency, "a peacetime organization which should be used in natural disasters even though it may never have to be used for war."[7] The Hopley report laid the groundwork for an institutionalized federal response to disasters. Soon after, the Disaster Relief Act of 1950 replaced ad hoc aid packages with general law governing disaster relief.[8] President Eisenhower issued the first presidential declaration of a major disaster in 1953 to help four counties in Georgia recover from a tornado.

Cold War emergency preparedness cultivated a shared sense of national risk by involving the public in preparation for nuclear war. The government funded large-scale programs, such as the construction of bomb shelters and the printing of instructional materials, but the thrust of the civil defense program was educating the public through the "militarization" of the home: Dad built a bomb shelter in the backyard, Mom prepared a survival kit, and the children learned to "duck and cover" at school.[9] The actual rate of participation in civil defense programs was relatively low, however. According to some studies at the time only 4.5% of U.S. citizens participated in civil defense programs.[10] Civil defense accomplished its goals more by cultivating awareness and a sense of shared risk than through active citizen participation.

Studies of citizen preparedness efforts criticized the U.S. effort for being ineffective and superficial. One prominent report noted, "Whether it was looked upon as 'insurance' or as playing a vital role in strategic deterrence, civil defense was never brought to a level of effort that would ensure substantial protection of the population, industry, and the economy in a nuclear assault."[11] Critics, however, overlooked the effort's most profound effects. Civil defense raised the salience of the Cold War for most individuals and involved citizens in preparedness efforts, whether or not civil defense would have significantly reduced losses during an attack. Natural disaster preparedness, in contrast, was largely the domain of government officials and specialized nonprofits, until a disaster occurred and individuals found themselves in dire straits. The basic organizational framework of civil defense in which the federal government provided loose coordination of state and local efforts continued to characterize emergency response in later years. Natural disaster preparedness, however, was not as prominent as civil defense during its peak, in part because natural disasters were seen as individual, isolated, and random acts of God, while civil defense was a national effort against a feared adversary.[12]

FROM AD HOC FEDERAL AID TO FEMA

By the 1970s, state and local governments had grown frustrated from navigating the many agencies responsible for elements of disaster preparedness. The Council of State Governments and the National Governors Association issued reports criticizing the "lack of a national policy for the management of natural, man-made, and attack emergencies."[13] States had trouble accessing assistance from the wide range of federal agencies responsible for disasters, many of which were either stovepipes focused on a single hazard or in turmoil because of internal organizational tension between civil defense and natural disaster cultures.

The gradual nationalization of disaster policy until the homeland security era provides a lens into how the American nation grew from one of dispersed regional responsibility to one in which the federal government assumed greater power over resources and policy while still ceding more authority to states and localities than many other nations. The federal government has provided a measure of relief from major disasters since the early days of the republic.[14] As the scope and resources of the national government grew, the federal government began to provide more money more frequently for disaster relief through greater appropriations and through reorganization, adding new agencies and programs in a piecemeal fashion. States and localities welcomed new resources, but their leaders grew frustrated with the scattered nature of federal disaster agencies and programs. The loudest call for the creation of a national agency to set disaster policy came from states and localities, who would nonetheless lose some authority in deciding how to prepare for and respond to disasters.

In 1979, President Carter created FEMA by executive order, giving the agency authority over emergency preparedness, fire prevention, civil defense disaster response, flood insurance, and continuity of government in case of nuclear attack. The new, independent agency reporting directly to the president and Congress was an amalgam of existing agencies and programs formerly housed in the Federal Communications Commission and the Departments of Housing and Urban Development, Commerce, and Defense. The idea of a single agency responsible for all types of disasters appealed to planners in Congress and the White House despite the uneasy relationship between civil defense and emergency managers. FEMA's first director, John Macy, faced the same challenges as earlier preparedness chiefs in attempting to unify efforts against many different kinds of hazards. Under his leadership, FEMA began development of an Integrated Emergency Management System that included "direction, control and warning systems which are common to the full range of emergencies from small isolated events to the ultimate emergency—war."[15]

As the Cold War waned, emergency managers dropped the term "dual use" in favor of "integrated emergency management" and then "all hazards" to describe the notion that, as much as possible, plans and equipment should be developed to address a range of hazards. This idea was just one among many in the policy stream, however, and it competed with the pet projects of divisions within FEMA, including bureaus responsible for earthquakes, fire hazards, and civil defense.

The creation of FEMA centralized previously scattered disaster agencies in a single organization devoted to the new principle of "emergency management" rather than the old approach of "civil defense," a change as significant as the more recent use of the term "homeland security." Emergency managers began to conceive of themselves as a profession in the 1980s, and journals, training programs, and college courses in the field slowly emerged. Partisans of emergency management might have thought that a single agency devoted to preparing for emergencies, of which natural disasters were the most frequent, would spell the end of preparation for deliberate attack outside the traditional military and security agencies. Several factors combined to maintain the strength of FEMA's national security and civil defense organizations, however.

Terrorism was a periodic concern throughout the 1970s, and the 1978 National Governors Association report that helped lead to the creation of FEMA found it one of the policy areas in need of better coordination.[16] Ronald Reagan took office in 1981 on a platform that emphasized the Soviet threat, and he installed Louis O. Giuffrida, a former National Guard officer and director of a state counterterrorism and emergency preparedness institute, as FEMA director. Meanwhile, Congress approved funding for a new civil defense initiative. Giuffrida envisioned FEMA as the lead agency for counterterrorism, riots, and domestic disturbances, and though FEMA could not compete with more powerful national security agencies, it maintained a well-funded and secretive national security division.[17]

In a gulf that foreshadowed tensions in the contemporary Department of Homeland Security (DHS), the division between security and non-security missions shortly after the creation of FEMA added to confusion about the purpose of emergency management among civil servants in a variety of disaster specialties. Political appointees lacked the expertise to settle these disputes and in many cases brought new priorities that compounded confusion. Carter's plan creating FEMA gave the agency eight political appointees at the outset, and by the end of the Carter administration the agency had thirty-one political appointees for approximately three thousand employees, one of the highest ratios in government. As a small coordinating agency, FEMA was not at the top of the Carter, Reagan, or George H. W. Bush agendas, nor was vetting its appointees. A House committee called FEMA a "federal turkey farm" because of its reputation as a dumping ground for political executives.[18]

The agency had multiple masters in Congress, deepening tensions among its multiple missions. FEMA reported to over a dozen congressional committees, including the Senate Armed Services Committee, which confirmed appointees to an associate director position in FEMA. Though formally committed to developing a single approach to preparing for emergencies, the agency was divided among civil defense and national security programs (and their congressional patrons), on one hand, and natural disaster programs, on the other, which included fiercely independent bureaus, such as the U.S. Fire Administration. With its missions confused and its programs in silos, FEMA had difficulty mounting effective responses to disasters.

Before the creation of FEMA, states and localities that experienced a catastrophic event looked to the federal government primarily for financial resources to help rebuild communities after the disaster struck. With the creation of FEMA, state and local authorities had a single source through which to request assistance — part of Carter's original plan — as well as a single agency to blame when disasters caught communities unprepared. FEMA made mistakes in its response efforts, but in many cases FEMA suffered blame for state and local failures over which it had little control. News stories rarely tracked the long, complicated process of establishing zoning regulations that might reduce the damage caused by disasters, but the media routinely covered major hurricanes, earthquakes, and floods. Local officials, the media, and members of Congress shifted blame from their own failures to prepare for disasters to FEMA's failure to respond quickly and forcefully enough.

Disaster aid has always been political in the sense that politicians derive electoral benefits from delivering resources to constituents and from assisting victims of high-profile events. Presidents from both parties have been increasingly likely over time to issue disaster declarations. From 1953 to 1969, Eisenhower, Kennedy, and Johnson averaged about 1.3 major disaster declarations per month; from 1989 to 2005, George H. W. Bush, Bill Clinton, and George W. Bush averaged 3.9 major disaster declarations per month. Economists Thomas Garrett and Russell Sobel have argued that from 1991 to 1999 states politically important to a sitting president had a higher rate of disaster declaration by the chief executive and that disaster expenditures were higher in states that had congressional representation on FEMA oversight committees.[19]

FEMA's poor performance in responding to a series of hurricanes in the late 1980s and early 1990s led some members of Congress to call for abolishing the agency. Rather than fold FEMA into another department, in 1993 new director James Lee Witt led a reorganization that demanded new independence for the agency and a newly focused disaster mission. With the advice of emergency management professional associations and a staff steeped in disaster work, Witt shrank the agency's top-secret national security division and obtained more resources to prepare for natural disasters more quickly.

In retrospect, it appears that FEMA's reputation had to hit bottom before the agency could achieve a consensus on how to reconcile its multiple missions and authorities. It is difficult to imagine the president, Congress, and the agency's many factions agreeing on a major reform if all the parties were not dissatisfied with the status quo and the agency did not face the threat of extinction. By 1992, FEMA's reputation and the morale of its employees had reached their nadirs, but the crisis created an opportunity. Senator Ernest Hollings called FEMA's staff "the sorriest bunch of bureaucratic jackasses [he'd] ever known" after the agency's poor performance responding to Hurricane Hugo in 1989.[20] FEMA's response to Hurricane Andrew in 1992 was so slow and so widely publicized as inadequate that President Bush, in the midst of an election campaign, sent nearly 20,000 navy, air force, and coast guard troops to Florida and asked the secretary of transportation to take charge.[21] Dade County emergency management director Kate Hale held a press conference in the midst of the Andrew aftermath in which she said: "Where the hell is the cavalry on this one? We need food. We need water. We need people.... For God's sake, where are they?"[22]

Faced with a media uproar, Congress convened blue-ribbon panels and began investigations into FEMA's performance. The chief culprit for FEMA's poor planning and slow response, the reports found, was its national security division, which set policies that hampered natural disaster relief. For example, FEMA developed a cutting-edge information technology system, but political executives refused to allow it to be used for disaster response because of national security concerns. The system would have proved useful in 1989 when the agency was overwhelmed with applications for assistance from victims of Hurricane Hugo and the Loma Prieto earthquake.[23] At that time, FEMA dedicated about 38% of its staff and about 27% of its budget (about $100 million, excluding the disaster relief fund) to national security emergencies.[24] Some of the agency's employees held security clearances while others did not, creating (at least) two competing cultures.

Drawing on expert reports, Witt proposed a reorganization of FEMA that unambiguously positioned the agency as the clearinghouse for natural disaster preparedness and relief programs. Witt reduced security clearances by 40% and moved national security programs for civil defense and continuity of government into a single, smaller division.[25] He made mitigation a central part of disaster preparedness and issued grants to states and localities to reduce risk before disasters struck by, for example, providing incentives to property owners to limit building in floodplains or to strengthen structures in earthquake zones. Studies show that a dollar spent on mitigation activities, such as strengthening building codes or relocating structures from floodplains, saves money that would have been spent on disaster response and recovery.[26]

The burgeoning emergency management profession, by then with regular conferences, academic researchers, and a few collegiate degree programs, offered the idea of "all hazards, all phases" as the intellectual centerpiece of the reorganization.[27] FEMA was a small coordinating agency with limited resources charged with an awesome task—preparation, response, and recovery for a range of disaster types. "All hazards" gave priority to programs that could be used for a range of disasters rather than a single type. Natural disasters had more in common with each other than with deliberate attack, and the "all hazards" organizing concept allowed the leaders of the FEMA reorganization to argue for more resources for natural disasters as an approach that provided more "bang for the buck" than civil defense and security programs.

The "all phases" portion of the concept attempted to involve the federal government before a disaster occurred in order to reduce vulnerabilities. It emphasized all four stages of the disaster timeline, including mitigation, preparation, response, and recovery. The agency formalized the concept when it developed federal response plans to coordinate duties in different disasters, and states and localities outlined plans along the same lines—essentially sidelining national security responsibilities and bringing natural disasters to the fore.

Congress passed legislation authorizing the reorganization that reduced the number of committees responsible for FEMA and the power held by national security committees as well as allowing FEMA to pre-position resources in anticipation of a disaster, without waiting for a hurricane, for example, to make landfall. The reorganization also granted FEMA more autonomy over policy decisions, and Witt eliminated ten presidentially appointed management posts in the agency. "The White House didn't like that," Witt said, referring to the Democratic Party operatives who staffed the Presidential Personnel Office, "but the president didn't mind."[28] Now reporting to fewer congressional committees, Witt's congressional relations office focused on educating key members of Congress about "all hazards, all phases" emergency management.

FEMA's reputation soared beginning in 1993, as it demoted its national security division and delivered more money to states and localities through mitigation programs. From 1995 to 2002, major newspaper editorials mentioning the agency were all either positive or neutral, while in previous years they were nearly all negative.[29] Media accounts captured the agency's improvements in preparation and response. While responding to floods in the Midwest in the summer of 1993, for example, FEMA used mobile communications vehicles that had previously been reserved for national security programs.

SOURCES OF ORGANIZATIONAL CHANGE

How did the agency accomplish such a remarkable turnaround, going from an object of derision on the floor of Congress and on late-night talk shows to one of the most popular agencies in government? An enterprising administrative politician, James Lee Witt used the knowledge and experience of the emergency management profession to give the agency a clear mission and improve its response to disasters. Disasters create communities of sufferers, and Witt offers a model for how entrepreneurial managers can structure organizations to serve these communities.

The challenge of transforming the Department of Homeland Security is greater than the challenge of transforming FEMA was in the 1990s because of the number of hazards and constituencies involved in the disparate field of "homeland security."[30] Nevertheless, reformers today should take note that Witt did not take the goals of his agency as a given but instead redefined what emergency management was about. The Witt-era FEMA took responsibility for preparing for disaster but avoided using intelligence to try to prevent attack, thus downgrading the agency's counterterrorism responsibility.

The term "disaster" is not self-evident, and social norms and the organization of government can affect what is considered a disaster.[31] For example, hurricanes count as disasters, while car accidents that occur over the course of a year do not. And deadly heat waves or droughts are only occasionally or after the fact referred to as disasters in the United States. The federal government is most concerned about preparing for disasters that are so rare that they overwhelm the capacities of state and local authorities. These disasters strike at an unpredictable time, inflict high and concentrated damage, and cause severe economic, social, and human costs in terms of lost economic productivity, social disruption, and loss of life.

Deliberate attacks can have consequences that resemble those of natural and technological disasters. A nuclear bomb could have some of the same effects as a nuclear power plant accident, and a terrorist attack against a dam could produce the same effects as a flood. *Preventing* a deliberate attack, however, whether terrorist or otherwise, requires a different approach than preparing for disasters. FEMA lacked the intelligence and law enforcement powers necessary to prevent attacks, but it risked being blamed for damage caused by nuclear attack or terrorism if it assumed responsibility for prevention and preparation rather than simply assisting in the response to an attack, as the agency did during Witt's tenure after the bombing of a federal building in Oklahoma City. Deliberate attacks were far too rare and unpredictable and FEMA's authority far too limited for Witt to want to make counterterrorism part of the agency's "brand" to the degree that Giuffrida had planned for FEMA earlier in the agency's history. When the Federal Response Plan, the principal federal document governing disaster response, gave terrorism crisis management responsibilities to the FBI (Federal Bureau of Investigation), Witt did not protest. Fifteen years earlier, FEMA's leadership had tussled with the bureau and the Justice Department over who would control crisis management during the aftermath of terrorism and civil disturbances, and the lines of authority were murky. During the Witt era, however, FEMA focused its mission on preparation, response, and recovery for natural disasters, and it played only a supportive role in terrorism and industrial disaster preparation and response.

Some theorists of bureaucracy posit that agencies seek "budget maximization" in order to expand resources and power indefinitely.[32] But FEMA's leaders resisted simple maximization, refusing to oversee some anti-terrorism programs in order to focus the agency's mission around natural disaster preparedness and response. Other scholars claim that agencies seek autonomy, or control over their mission and resources, so that they are able to use their expertise to satisfy a public need.[33] FEMA's history best suits the autonomy model. Over time, leaders worked with Congress, emergency management professionals, and the staff of several presidential administrations to match the agency's capacities to an achievable mission. Reducing the power of FEMA's national security division and giving more authority to programs devoted to natural hazards were essential to the reorganization. In addition, the agency reduced the number of political appointees and the number of congressional committees to which it reported, giving more power to career civil servants.

The new Mitigation Directorate was a centerpiece of the reorganized FEMA, providing grants to states and localities to reduce vulnerability to hazards through moving structures, improving defenses, and other measures. If successful, reduced vulnerability to hazards would make response and recovery easier. In practice, mitigation wavered between being a program of free-flowing federal grants with few strings and a program to educate public officials and private citizens about how to protect themselves against disasters and, only when absolutely necessary, to provide them with financial assistance for specific projects.[34] The Bush administration deemphasized mitigation out of concerns that such programs were open to waste, fraud, and abuse.

Measuring the value of mitigation programs proves difficult because it requires accounting for non-events, but in this respect it is no different than regulating for other safety and security measures. Recent attempts to document the value of mitigation show that well-implemented mitigation programs reduce the damage caused by inevitable fires, floods, earthquakes, and other disasters.[35] The most comprehensive study, by the Multihazard Mitigation Council of the National Institute of Building Sciences, found that on average a dollar spent by FEMA on hazard mitigation provides about $4 in future benefits as well as saving lives.[36] To the extent that mitigation promotes a sustainable or resilient natural environment, it has benefits that are not adequately evaluated by economic measures. For example, preventing severe drought preserves fish, forests, and other wildlife and natural ecosystems that might otherwise be damaged.[37]

Though mitigation may be useful for defending against terrorist attacks — structural mitigation prevented the attack on the Pentagon on September 11 from being worse than it was — during the 1990s mitigation programs focused primarily on natural hazards. Creating a mitigation directorate moved the agency away from national security functions toward natural hazards that are more easily mitigated than prevented.

EMERGENCY MANAGEMENT IN A
HOMELAND SECURITY ENVIRONMENT

Almost a decade after FEMA's reorganization, the agency underwent another remarkable turnaround — in the other direction. After a change in presidential administrations and then the terrorist attacks of 2001, a new FEMA leadership looked for a way to organize the federal role in disasters around a security mission. During the transition, morale plummeted, and many positions in the agency went unfilled. FEMA was famously criticized for a poor response to Hurricane Katrina in 2005 as well as for waste, fraud, and mismanagement, though in Katrina there was plenty of blame to go around among agencies and individuals at all levels of government. By 2005, FEMA's capacity had deteriorated. The agency's attempt at defining its mission to match its capacities had fallen victim to two forces in contemporary government — bureaucratization and politicization.

Bureaucratization, sometimes known as the "thickening of government," refers to the growth in both the number of people in government and the layers of hierarchy that separate them.[38] The federal government has fifteen departments headed by Senate-confirmed presidential appointees — secretaries, deputy secretaries, under secretaries, and administrators. Each of these executives has a staff of senior executives, which includes chiefs of staff, associate deputy secretaries, assistant under secretaries, deputy assistant secretaries, and associate administrators. These men and women, appointees and civil servants, are the senior executives that make policy for the bureaucracy. The number of senior executives has increased from 451 in 1960 to 2,409 in 1992; 2,385 in 1998; and 2,595 in 2004.[39] The number may grow in proportion to increasing government responsibility or because of politicians' and public managers' desires for control. Whatever the cause, the kudzu-like growth of political executives makes navigating the bureaucracy an increasingly complex endeavor.[40]

While a desire for control and improved performance motivates bureaucratization, this "thickening" of government paradoxically frustrates control and accountability. After September 11, the Department of Homeland Security was created to refocus the bureaucracy around terrorism-related missions to correct the perceived organizational failures leading up to the attacks. The department absorbed FEMA as well as twenty-one other agencies responsible for missions other than terrorism, including customs inspection and fisheries protection. Political scientist Mariano Florentino-Cuéllar shows how new terrorism missions detracted from the coast guard's other legacy missions.[41] Others have blamed the focus on terrorism for FEMA's shortcomings in Katrina. Representative Bill Shuster claimed that DHS leaders allowed FEMA's capacities to deteriorate "because its disaster mission cannot compete with DHS' terrorism prevention mission."[42] This view sees prevention and interdiction of attack as categorically different from other "all hazards, all phases" preparedness tasks, overwhelming other concerns when included in the same agency.

Some observers speculated that the Bush administration intended to shrink the non-security missions of homeland security agencies in order to fulfill a longstanding agenda to reduce the federal government's role in domestic policy.[43] In addition to bureaucratization, Congress and the executive attempted to politicize FEMA, or substitute their policy preferences for those of career civil servants. The chief vehicles for politicization are appointments, policy statements, and reorganization. Joseph Allbaugh, the political campaign manager whom George W. Bush selected to replace Witt as FEMA director, began his tenure by reducing mitigation programs and proposing new programs for terrorism preparedness. September 11 catalyzed the trend toward a terrorism-focused mission, and a new class of political appointees at FEMA ensured that the agency would revise its policies.

Critics blame much of FEMA's poor performance on politicization.[44] The agency had thirty-five political appointees by the end of George H. W. Bush's term, but after the agency's reorganization during the Clinton presidency, it had only twenty-two. By 2002, however, that number had grown to thirty-eight. Appointees filled top management positions, policy development and speechwriting jobs, and some presumably technical jobs in newly created positions in the External Affairs Directorate and Information Technology Services. Whereas many of the Witt-era appointees had long careers in emergency management, the George W. Bush administration filled FEMA's upper management with political appointees who lacked disaster experience.[45] In addition to FEMA director Michael Brown's much-lampooned prior experience as a lawyer with the International Arabian Horse Association, as of September 2005 other agency leaders lacked emergency management credentials before their FEMA appointments: the chief of staff, Patrick Rhode, formerly planned events for Bush's campaign; the deputy chief of staff, Scott Morris, was previously a media strategist for Bush campaigns. Neither had previous emergency management experience.

By then, FEMA's political appointees had to work through DHS appointees, and bureaucratization and politicization combined to make it difficult for career civil servants in FEMA to influence broad policy. The Witt-led reorganization drew on the knowledge of the emergency management profession to expand mitigation programs to reduce disaster risk and recommend the "all hazards" approach to get the most out of limited resources and claim authority for natural disaster preparedness against civil defense. By the time Katrina struck, however, FEMA professionals faced layers of political management, a political agenda that emphasized the terrorist threat, and entrenched state and local authority over disaster preparedness.

LESSONS FOR PUBLIC MANAGERS

Over time, the national government has assumed responsibility for reducing risk in many realms of life. Disasters are no exception. Much of the authority for risk reduction, however, rests with states, localities, and private citizens who make decisions about construction, settlement patterns, and evacuation. FEMA is in a difficult position. It can claim credit and win accolades for successful disaster preparedness and response, but it lacks the capacity to prevent and protect against major disasters without partners in state and local governments, private industry, and nonprofits. Few of FEMA's partners, however, recognize the extent to which the agency depends on other actors for achieving success.

After a period of poor performance and threatened with abolition, FEMA's leadership constructed a niche for the agency as the major natural disaster preparedness and response organization. The agency has some power to shape what constitutes a "disaster" or "event" deemed worthy of federal response, but FEMA is also at the mercy of larger trends. September 11 raised the salience of terrorism, and a reorganization left FEMA under the larger Department of Homeland Security, where many of its grants, organizations, and staff were restructured to address terrorism.

Disaster planners can look to the recent past to understand how FEMA might cope with impossible expectations for disaster preparedness. FEMA's resources were most closely aligned with its mission during the Witt era. The agency had an administrative politician who bridged the gaps among several groups. He connected civil servants to elected politicians by building strong relationships with each. He convinced politicians that a relatively independent disaster agency that drew on the resources of the emergency management profession would serve their interests through effective disaster preparedness for which politicians could claim credit. He listened to career bureaucrats and incorporated their ideas in policy planning. To strengthen the agency's influence over states and localities, Witt established a mitigation grant program that rewarded governments and property owners for actions taken to reduce disaster risk. FEMA also simplified the disaster assistance process by providing toll-free numbers, and Witt asked members of Congress to call him personally if they had concerns. State emergency managers praised these efforts. One said, "This is the first time we have had this coordination in my experience.... They think like we do."[46]

Successful emergency response requires more than a particular organizational form. People understand events through different "ways of knowing," and effective public policy acknowledges the differences in how people interpret events that are at the root of apparent disagreements.[47] Everyone agrees that hurricane protection is a desirable end, but because actors have different understandings of what a hurricane means, they disagree about policy. To coastal property owners, a hurricane is a threat to their property. To meteorologists, it is a natural event that makes landfall in the United States roughly five times every three years. To oil companies drilling in the Gulf of Mexico, it is a risk to business and a potential interruption of service. Public managers must first ask how members of a policy network come to know what an event means before they can craft a policy solution that speaks to everyone who might be affected.

EMERGENCY MANAGEMENT IN A NETWORK ENVIRONMENT

The peculiar institutional history of emergency management in the United States creates challenges not faced by other countries where disaster policy is more centralized. Nevertheless, the strategies for managing a fluid U.S. network of emergency management organizations are relevant for the even more diffuse international context. Development patterns contribute to increased disaster losses, but the authority to reduce these losses is diffuse. In the United States, emergency preparedness is primarily the responsibility of states, localities, and private citizens. The national government has had only a weak, coordinative role, even as expectations about Washington, DC's responsibilities in disaster policy have grown. The decentralized nature of emergency management coupled with the national government's relatively weak role provides an opportunity for FEMA to be an important node in coordinating a diffuse network.

There are several reasons why the national government should be involved rather than leaving preparedness to states alone or individual citizens. Psychologists show that people tend to underestimate their exposure to many low-probability, high-consequence events while over-estimating their exposure to events like those in recent memory.[48] Furthermore, the probability of catastrophic disasters is uncertain, which frustrates efforts at rational planning.[49] Finally, in many cases, the federal government's land-use policies contribute to vulnerability, and the federal government bears responsibility for its contribution to creating disaster. For example, the Army Corps of Engineers completed a seventy-six-mile canal, the Mississippi River–Gulf Outlet (MR–GO), in the 1960s as a shortcut for ships traveling from the river to the gulf. Studies of Hurricane Katrina show that it served as a funnel increasing the velocity of storm surges into New Orleans.[50]

Disaster preparedness and response occur through actors who rely on each other but are not subject to direct control. FEMA commands many of the headlines when a disaster occurs, but a study of the response to the terrorist attacks on the World Trade Center puts the agency's role in perspective. A total of 1,607 organizations participated in the response, and of these 1,196 were nonprofits and 149 were private firms.[51] Organizations with well-rehearsed plans seemed to perform well, but the event was so unexpected and the response so large that it could never be rehearsed precisely.[52] The relevant actors appeared to understand their roles and adapt their responses energetically if not spontaneously. Charities, for example, devoted resources to helping victims' families and to helping New Yorkers cope with the trauma of a direct attack.

Critics of the federal government's comparatively diminished role in public action label contemporary government a "hollow state."[53] FEMA, like other agencies, contributes to the "hollow state" by locating much of its capacity outside government, as when it enters into contracts with private firms to provide public services. These firms create a state within the state, a network of firms whose employees are not subject to government regulations but who perform functions once carried out by federal employees. Blackwater USA, a security firm hired by the DHS to protect areas ravaged by Katrina, receives 90% of its revenues from state government contracts, and the majority of its employees once worked for government.[54] Proponents of "contracting out" claim that private firms are more flexible and adaptable than government agencies, while critics complain that private firms are less accountable and contribute to the weakening of government capacity because their employees are more transient.[55]

In the years before Katrina, retirements, vacancies, and contracts with private firms hollowed out FEMA's core. By 2005, the agency had only 2,500 full-time employees and a vacancy rate of 15% to 20% that left the agency unable to handle the surge in capacity demanded during a catastrophe.[56] After Katrina, Congress approved $62 billion for food, water, shelter, transportation, and other relief items. The aid needed to be distributed immediately, but FEMA had only approximately fifty acquisitions personnel. In one of its first post-disaster actions, the agency hired a firm, Acquisition Solutions, to draft contracts. The contractor employed many former FEMA employees who were familiar with emergency management, but the speed with which FEMA awarded this and other contracts made the agency susceptible to charges of favoritism, waste, and lack of oversight in its Katrina contracts.[57]

It is worth putting concerns about the hollow state in perspective. Disaster management in the United States has always existed in a networked environment in which the federal government was a minor player. FEMA and its predecessors have always navigated shared, overlapping responsibility for hazards among federal, state, and local entities.[58] And despite its problems, public-private cooperation can be more flexible than centralized control. A network can more easily adapt to new conditions than a hierarchy if its nodes are given enough independence, shared goals, and trust.[59] (Networks also require structures of accountability, or they risk incoherence.)

For example, the rapid, multiorganizational response to the September 11 attacks at the World Trade Center site was judged a success. Like other networked emergency management efforts, the response succeeded because the organizations involved had a high degree of trust cultivated through long, collaborative relationships. The networked environment also explains why James Lee Witt's activist, collaborative, and connected management style succeeded. The best public managers in a networked environment are "administrative politicians" who routinely communicate shared goals to constituencies in and out of government.[60] The professions at the core of the agency's function provide a key vehicle for coordination and understanding across levels of government and among the private sector, universities, and nonprofits that neither pure centralization nor total privatization can provide.

EMERGENCY PREPAREDNESS AND THE PRIVATIZATION OF RISK

Defining an event as a "disaster" spreads risk and responsibility by forging a community of sufferers. The history of the increasing national role in disaster response and, more recently, disaster prevention, protection, and mitigation is a history of increasingly shared responsibility for risk driven by calls from citizens as well as subnational governments for greater federal involvement. The national government now delivers more money and assistance for victims of more kinds of disasters than ever before. At the same time, the burden of disaster risk still falls heavily on individuals. The rich and well-connected can afford to bear risk and either sustain losses or organize to obtain government aid for recovery, while the poor and socially isolated are more likely to be devastated by disaster. Shifting the burden of disaster from collective organizations of government to private individuals is the central meaning of "privatization," which can take many forms, from contracting out government services to be performed by private firms to the increased use of private markets for social insurance.

Since the early days of the republic, disasters have been a national concern because they spill across state lines and can overwhelm state and local authorities. Ardent libertarians might recommend that states form compacts to cooperate in providing emergency assistance in the absence of national resources. But if all states joined in a compact, they would act just like a national government. The Articles of Confederation operated through agreements among states, but the arrangement proved too weak. Today, states only rarely agree on mutual assistance compacts, probably because of high transaction costs. The national government can set standards and coordinate assistance in a cheaper and more effective way than agreements among fifty states.

While coordinating disaster preparedness should be a national if not international effort involving many levels of government and private entities, any level of government intervention that increases vulnerability is a concern. Recovery aid that, for example, helps people rebuild in floodplains or dense forests uses public money to subsidize risk for which only private citizens, typically home or business owners, reap the rewards. The threat of disaster is increasing as Americans build more valuable structures in more vulnerable places than ever before.

Individuals under-prepare for natural disasters because these hazards are what Peter Huber labels a "public risk." These "are centrally produced or mass-produced, broadly distributed, often temporally remote, and largely outside the individual risk bearer's direct understanding and control."[61] Public risks are either high-probability, low-consequence events or low-probability, high-consequence events for which there is little incentive to engage in collective action without a dramatic focusing event such as a major disaster. Private risks, in contrast, have either moderate probability or moderate consequences, and thus, people are more likely to take steps to mitigate them, such as fixing a roof leak.

Public risks, such as natural disasters or, without a focusing event, terrorist attacks, go unaddressed because they are outside the individual experience of daily life. They appear remote, if they are comprehended at all. As a result, citizens as individuals do little to organize to prepare for disaster. Nonprofits and private businesses face the same public risk problem and often fail to organize preparedness. Even experts and public officials failed to take the risk of a major terrorist attack in the United States seriously until after September 11, even though the risk was well known.

The national government provides a valuable service when it institutionalizes preparation for public risks. While some critics complain that the reorganization that produced the DHS was too large, in hindsight it may not have been large enough in scope. A national department could have been charged with reducing a panoply of risks, including terrorism and even scientific and industrial disasters, as well as with supporting states and localities.[62] Some procedures could successfully be "all hazards," such as preparedness efforts and mitigating social vulnerabilities, while others would be more specialized, such as the use of intelligence to prevent attack. If the DHS is to move toward a more "all hazards" approach, it needs to develop methods, such as risk and vulnerability assessment, to help allocate resources and attention among threats.

The public, through state and local officials and fueled by the media, demands increased national responsibility for managing disasters that are often exacerbated by government policy. The national government's role has always been much smaller than the collective role of states, localities, and private citizens in emergency management. Privatization actually increases the need for government coordination (though not direct control) over the growing network of organizations responsible for emergency management. Government contracts with private firms to provide public services are intended to improve efficiency and expand capacity, but contracts alone cannot address vulnerabilities at the root of increasing disaster losses. The DHS could learn a lesson from the past by matching its missions with capabilities, as FEMA accomplished, albeit briefly, in the 1990s. The DHS faces a choice similar to FEMA's: it can put defense against deliberate attack at the heart of its mission or expand its responsibilities to include mitigating and preventing the most costly and catastrophic threats of all kinds. To do so, national authorities must learn that they exercise greater authority when they clarify the missions and practices of emergency management and leverage the expertise of professionals and subnational governments than when they attempt regulation or operational control.

For now, the tasks of preparation, response, and recovery rest with myriad organizations that are only loosely coordinated. As a result, long-term efforts to reduce disaster risk are haphazard, and the effectiveness of government response and recovery efforts is unpredictable and varies by region. After 2001, FEMA's capacity to organize disaster preparedness and response deteriorated. FEMA's rise and fall poses a puzzle for social science: why did elected politicians contribute to the diminished capacity of an agency that provided them with electoral benefits? The cynical answer is that agencies are designed to fail by narrow-minded politicians and bureaucrats who fail to consider broad national concerns.[63] Another possibility, explored in this chapter, is that achieving "success" in coordinating emergency management is difficult for a small agency in a complex and changing environment without the cooperation of other actors.

Even more puzzling than the goals of elected politicians is the result of FEMA's diminished capacity for American society. After a century of increasing public responsibility for disaster risk, an ineffective FEMA, by default, places more responsibility for disaster risk in the hands of subnational governments and individuals. As a result, states, localities, and individuals with limited financial and cognitive resources focus on responding to the most severe and the most recent disasters. Without an effective national coordinating agency, long-term efforts to reduce the damage caused by either frequent but low-consequence events or rare but catastrophic disasters will get short shrift, and disaster losses will grow.

NOTES

1   E. L. Quarantelli, ed., *Disasters: Theory and Research* (Beverly Hills, CA: Sage Publications, 1978).

2   Issued by the White House after Hurricane Katrina, the *Lessons Learned* report recommends that emergency management functions be centralized like the structure of the Department of Defense. Francis Fragos Townsend, *The Federal Response*

to *Hurricane Katrina: Lessons Learned*, special White House report prepared by the assistant to the president for homeland security and counterterrorism, at the request of the president, February 2006.

3   Naomi Klein, "Disaster Capitalism: The New Economy of Catastrophe," *Harper's Magazine*, October 2007, 47–58; and Jacob S. Hacker, *The Great Risk Shift: The Assault on American Jobs, Families, Health Care and Retirement and How You Can Fight Back* (Oxford: Oxford University Press, 2006).

4   On the transition costs associated with reorganization, see Karen M. Hult, *Agency Merger and Bureaucratic Redesign* (Pittsburgh, PA: University of Pittsburgh Press, 1987).

5   National Security Resources Board, "Preliminary Statement on Guiding Principles and Program Framework for Mobilization Planning," White House Central Files, Box 27, NSRB Folder 1, NSRB Doc. 76, August 19, 1948, http://www.trumanlibrary.org/hstpaper/whcfcf.htm; and Harry S. Truman, "Memorandum on Civil Defense Planning: March 4, 1949," American Presidency Project, http://www.presidency.ucsb.edu/ws/index.php?pid=13399.

6   Andrew D. Grossman, *Neither Dead Nor Red: Civilian Defense and American Political Development During the Early Cold War* (New York: Routledge, 2001), 54–57, 142; United Press, "Defense Lack Seen as 'Pearl Harbor,'" *New York Times*, October 10, 1949; *New York Times*, "Baruch is Critical of Defense Plans," October 31, 1949; and Joint Committee on Atomic Energy, *Civil Defense Against Atomic Attack: Hearings*, 81st Congress, 2d sess., 1950, 140–50.

7   Russell J. Hopley, *Civil Defense for National Security*, report to the secretary of defense by the Office of Civil Defense Planning, October 1, 1948, quoted in Jerry Conley, "The Role of the U.S. Military in Domestic Emergency Management: The Past, Present and Future," *EMSE 232 Disaster Newsletter* (George Washington University Institute for Crisis, Disaster, and Risk Management) 3, no. 4 (January 2003). Also see National Security Resources Board, "Progress Report on Civil Defense Planning Under the N.S.R.B. March 3, 1949–March 3, 1950," NSRB, Box 94, Folder E4-12, National Archives. For studies of early civil defense programs, see Nehemiah Jordan, *U.S. Civil Defense before 1950: The Roots of Public Law 920* (Arlington, VA: Institute for Defense Analyses, May 1966). Various civil defense leaders recall that the earliest conceptions of civil defense included defense against natural disasters; for example, civil defense agencies during the Truman administration cooperated with the General Services Administration to share knowledge about how to fight fires. See Richard Gerstell, "State Civil Defense Plans and Programs" (lecture, Industrial College of the Armed Forces, Washington, DC, October 22, 1963).

8   Thomas A. Birkland, *After Disaster: Agenda Setting, Public Policy, and Focusing Events* (Washington, DC: Georgetown University Press, 1997), 49–50.

9   Laura McEnaney, *Civil Defense Begins at Home: Militarization Meets Everyday Life in the Fifties* (Princeton, NJ: Princeton University Press, 2000); and Elaine Tyler May, *Homeward Bound: American Families in the Cold War Era* (New York: Basic Books, 1990).

10 Eric Klinenberg, "Are You Ready for the Next Disaster?" *New York Times Magazine*, July 6, 2008.

11 Harry B. Yoshpe, *Our Missing Shield: The U.S. Civil Defense Program in Historical Perspective* (Washington, DC: FEMA, April 1981), iv.

12 Stephen J. Collier and Andrew Lakoff, "Distributed Preparedness: Space, Security, and Citizenship in the United States," in *War, Citizenship, Territory*, ed. Deborah Cowen and Emily Gilbert (New York: Routledge, 2008), chap. 6.

13 Claire B. Rubin, ed., *Emergency Management: The American Experience 1900–2005* (Fairfax, VA: Public Entity Risk Institute, 2007), 102.

14 Michele Landis Dauber, "The Sympathetic State," *Law and History Review* 23, no. 2 (Summer 2005); and Michelle Landis Dauber, "Let Me Next Time Be 'Tried by Fire': Disaster Relief and the Origins of the American Welfare State 1789–1874," *Northwestern Law Review* 92 (Spring 1998): 967–1034.

15 Federal Emergency Management Agency, "FEMA History," http://www.fema.gov/about/history.shtm (accessed November 12, 2003).

16 National Governors' Association, *1978 Emergency Preparedness Project — Final Report* (Washington, DC: NGA, 1978), 107.

17 Charles Perrow, *The Next Catastrophe: Reducing Our Vulnerabilities to Natural, Industrial, and Terrorist Disasters* (Princeton, NJ: Princeton University Press, 2007), 55–58.

18 Larry Van Dyne, "Perfect Places for Those Hard-to-Place Contributors," *Washingtonian*, November 1992.

19 Thomas A. Garrett and Russell S. Sobel, "The Political Economy of FEMA Disaster Payments," *Economic Inquiry* 41, no. 3 (July 2003): 496–503. Other studies have found that a president's decision to issue a disaster declaration is influenced by congressional and media attention. See Richard T. Sylves, "The Politics and Budgeting of Federal Emergency Management," in *Disaster Management in the U.S. and Canada: The Politics, Policymaking, Administration and Analysis of Emergency Management*, ed. Richard T. Sylves and William L. Waugh, Jr. (Springfield, IL: Charles C. Thomas, 1996), 26–45.

20 James N. Baker, Howard Manly, and Daniel Glick, "The Storm After Hugo,"

Newsweek, October 9, 1989, 40; and *Economist*, "When the Wind Blows," September 30, 1989.

21 Bob Davis, "Brewing Storm: Federal Relief Agency Is Slowed by Infighting, Patronage, Regulations," *Wall Street Journal*, August 31, 1992. In addition, Wendy Brown emphasizes the "popular and media discourse about relevant state and federal agencies (e.g., the Federal Emergency Management Agency [FEMA]), that came close to displacing onto the agencies themselves responsibility for the suffering of victims." Wendy Brown, *States of Injury: Power and Freedom in Late Modernity* (Princeton, NJ: Princeton University Press, 1995), 68–69.

22 Peter Slevin and Dexter Filkins, "We Need Help," *Miami Herald*, August 28, 1992.

23 Robert Ward et al., "Network Organizational Development in the Public Sector: A Case Study of the Federal Emergency Management Agency (FEMA)," *Journal of the American Society of Information Science* 51, no. 11 (2000): 1018–32.

24 National Academy of Public Administration, *Coping with Catastrophe* (Washington, DC, February 1993), 53–54.

25 Richard G. Trefry, *Security Practices Board of Review Final Report and Recommendations* (Washington, DC: FEMA, November 1992); and Federal Emergency Management Agency, "Which FEMA Personnel Should Be Required to Have Security Clearances to Fulfill Their Emergency Assignments?" (deputy associate director memorandum, December 18, 1986).

26 Multihazard Mitigation Council, *Natural Hazard Mitigation Saves: An Independent Study to Address the Future Savings from Mitigation Activities* (Washington, DC: National Institute of Building Sciences, 2005), http://www.nibs.org/MMC/mmcactiv5.html; International Federation of Red Cross and Red Crescent Societies (IFRC), *Measuring Mitigation: Methodologies for Assessing Natural Hazard Risks and the Net Benefits of Mitigation* (Geneva: ProVention Consortium, 2004); and Hank Jenkins-Smith and Howard Kunreuther, "Mitigation and Benefits Measures as Policy Tools for Siting Potentially Hazardous Facilities: Determinants of Effectiveness and Appropriateness," *Risk Analysis* 21, no. 2 (April 2001): 371–82.

27 Patrick S. Roberts, "FEMA and the Prospects for Reputation-Based Autonomy," *Studies in American Political Development* 20, no. 1 (April 2006): 57–87; Wayne Blanchard, FEMA's Higher Education Project file and personal communication, June 4, 2005; and Arthur Oyola-Yemaiel and Jennifer Wilson, "Three Essential Strategies for Emergency Management Professionalization in the U.S.," *International Journal of Mass Emergencies and Disasters* 23, no. 1 (March 2005): 77–84.

28 James Lee Witt, personal interview with the author, April 15, 2004, Washington, DC.

29 Roberts, "FEMA and the Prospects."

30 Peter J. May, Joshua Sapotichne, and Samuel Workman, "Homeland Security: More or Less Coherent?" (paper presented at the annual meeting of the American Political Science Association, Chicago, August 28 – September 2, 2007).

31 Mariano-Florentino Cuéllar, "'Securing' the Bureaucracy: The Federal Security Agency and the Political Design of Legal Mandates, 1939–1953," Working Paper No. 943084 (Stanford Public Law, 2006).

32 William A. Niskanen, Jr., *Bureaucracy and Representative Government* (Chicago: Aldine Atherton, 1971).

33 Daniel P. Carpenter, *The Forging of Bureaucratic Autonomy: Reputations, Networks, and Policy Innovation in Executive Agencies, 1862–1928* (Princeton, NJ: Princeton University Press, 2001); and Roberts, "FEMA and the Prospects."

34 Rutherford H. Platt and Claire B. Rubin, "Stemming the Losses: The Quest for Hazard Mitigation," in *Disasters and Democracy: The Politics of Extreme Natural Events*, ed. Rutherford H. Platt (Washington, DC: Island Press, 1999), 69–110.

35 IFRC, *Measuring Mitigation*; and Jenkins-Smith and Kunreuther, "Mitigation and Benefits Measures."

36 Multihazard Mitigation Council, *Natural Hazard Mitigation Saves.*

37 Peter H. Gleick and Linda Nash, "The Societal and Environmental Costs of the Continuing California Drought," (Berkeley, CA: Pacific Institute for Studies in Development, Environment, and Security, 1991).

38 Paul C. Light, *Thickening Government: Federal Hierarchy and the Diffusion of Accountability* (Washington, DC: Brookings Institution Press, 1995).

39 Paul C. Light, "Fact Sheet on the Continued Thickening of Government," Brookings Institution, July 23, 2004.

40 James Q. Wilson, *Bureaucracy* (New York: Basic Books, 2000), 11–12, 218–20.

41 Mariano Florentino-Cuéllar, "Running Aground: The Hidden Environmental and Regulatory Implications of Homeland Security," Issue Brief (American Constitution Society for Law and Policy, May 2007).

42 Quoted in Tim Starks, "Fixing FEMA: A Flurry of Ideas to Address Autonomy, Control and Purpose," *CQ Homeland Security*, April 27, 2006: 1–3, http://homeland. cq.com/hs/display.do?dockey=/cqonline/prod/data/docs/html/news/109/ news109-000002166895.html@allnewsarchive&metapub=CQNEWS&seqNum= 2&searchIndex=6.

43 Dara Kay Cohen, Mariano-Florentino Cuéllar, and Barry R. Weingast, "Crisis Bureaucracy: Homeland Security and the Political Design of Legal Mandates," *Stanford Law Review* 59, no. 3 (2006): 673–759.

44 David Lewis, *The Politics of Presidential Appointments: Political Control and*

Bureaucratic Performance (Princeton, NJ: Princeton University Press, forthcoming).

45 Spencer S. Hsu, "Leaders Lacking Disaster Experience," *Washington Post*, September 9, 2005.

46 Vernon Hyse, "High Marks for FEMA—For Now," *CQ Weekly*, July 17, 1993.

47 Martha S. Feldman and Anne M. Khademian, "The Role of the Public Manager in Inclusion: Creating Communities of Participation," *Governance* 20, no. 2 (April 2007): 305–24.

48 Robert J. Meyer, "Why We Under-Prepare for Hazards," in *On Risk and Disaster: Lessons from Hurricane Katrina*, ed. Ronald J. Daniels, Donald F. Kettl, and Howard Kunreuther (Philadelphia: University of Pennsylvania Press, 2006), 153–74.

49 Richard A. Posner, *Catastrophe: Risk and Response* (New York: Oxford University Press, 2004).

50 Christopher Cooper and Robert Block, *Disaster: Hurricane Katrina and the Failure of Homeland Security* (New York: Times Books, 2006), 26–28.

51 Naim Kapucu, "Interagency Communication Networks During Emergencies: Boundary Spanners in Multiagency Coordination, *American Review of Public Administration* 36 (2006): 207–225, 213.

52 U.S. General Accounting Office, *September 11: Interim Report on the Response of Charities*, GAO-02-1037 (Washington, DC, September 2002); and U.S. General Accounting Office, *September 11: Overview of Federal Disaster Assistance to the New York City Area*, GAO-04-72 (Washington, DC, October 2003), 13–34.

53 H. Brinton Milward and Keith G. Provan, "Governing the Hollow State," *Journal of Public Administration Research and Theory* 10, no. 2 (April 2000): 359–80.

54 Klein, "Disaster Capitalism"; and Bill Sizemore and Joanne Kimberline, "Blackwater: On the Front Lines," *Virginian-Pilot*, July 25, 2006.

55 Eric Klinenberg and Thomas Frank, "Looting Homeland Security," *Rolling Stone*, December 29, 2005, 44–54.

56 Senate Committee on Homeland Security and Governmental Affairs, *Hurricane Katrina: A Nation Still Unprepared*, 109th Cong., 2d sess., 2006, S. Rpt. 109-322, chap. 14.

57 Griff Witte and Charles R. Babcock, "A Major Test for FEMA And Its Contracting Crew," *Washington Post*, September 13, 2005; and Griff Witte and Robert O'Harrow, "Short-Staffed FEMA Farms Out Procurement," *Washington Post*, September 17, 2005. To improve its surge capacity, FEMA could maintain a registry of pre-screened contractors with standing orders to provide services after a disaster.

58 Patrick S. Roberts, "Dispersed Federalism as a New Regional Governance for Homeland Security," *Publius: The Journal of Federalism* 38, no. 3 (2008): 416–43.

59 Max Stephenson, "Bridging the Organizational Divide: A Comparative Institutional Analysis of United States and International Humanitarian Service Delivery Structures," *Voluntas* 18, no. 3 (September 2007): 209–24.

60 Roberts, "FEMA and the Prospects."

61 Peter W. Huber, "The Bhopalization of American Tort Law," in *Hazards: Technology and Fairness*, National Academy of Engineering (Washington, DC: National Academies Press, 1986), 89–110.

62 Posner, *Catastrophe: Risk and Response.*

63 Amy Zegart, *Flawed By Design: The Evolution of the CIA, JCS, and NSC* (Palo Alto, CA: Stanford University Press, 1999).

CHAPTER THREE

Strange Brew | *Private Military Contractors and Humanitarians*

P. W. SINGER

In Afghanistan, a private demining team clears decades-old minefields so that local villagers can till their fields. In Iraq, a unit of corporate commandos escorts an engineering team fixing local sewage facilities. In Darfur, private helicopter crews provide transport for African peacekeepers. In the Democratic Republic of the Congo (DRC), private soldiers guard United Nations (UN) facilities and warehouses. And along the U.S. Gulf Coast, ravaged by Hurricane Katrina, privately contracted soldiers guard buildings from looters, rescue stranded families by helicopter, and collect and process the dead.

Scenes like these may have once sounded like fiction, but they are the new reality of intervention in all its forms in the twenty-first century. Humanitarian operations have undergone immense changes in recent decades, and perhaps one of the more notable developments has been the entry of hired military services, better known as the "privatized military industry," into the aid sphere. But it is also one of the least understood.

Privatized military firms (PMFs) are companies that provide professional military skills; they conduct tactical combat operations and strategic planning, offer troop training and technical assistance, and provide intelligence, operational, and logistics support.[1] Organized as business entities and structured along corporate lines, PMFs represent the evolution and corporatization of the older mercenary trade.[2] In some ways, this trend in defense contracting mirrors broader global economic changes, as industries shift from manufacturing to services and countries increasingly outsource functions once considered the preserve of the state. Yet, unlike any other aspect of human conduct, warfare is not mere business as usual.

The following text explores this strange new brew, laying out what is happening with private military firms and the humanitarian field today, highlighting some of the most important tensions and problems that occur when these two worlds come crashing together, exploring the rising question of domestic humanitarian operations, and finally, suggesting some ways that PMF clients, like humanitarian organizations, can better manage such tensions.

THE PRIVATE MILITARY INDUSTRY EXPLAINED

The private military industry rose from changes in the supply and demand forces behind the global security market at the end of the Cold War. With more than six million soldiers demobilized, military labor prices went down, and massive stocks of weapons fell into private hands, while the number of areas of instability and conflict has doubled. Meanwhile, changes in the modes of warfare increasingly blurred the lines between soldiers and civilians, while the growing privatization of state services provided an ideological climate for privatized military services.[3] Over the last ten years, PMFs have operated in over fifty countries and have been decisive actors in numerous conflicts, including Angola, Croatia, Ethiopia-Eritrea, and Sierra Leone. Even the U.S. military became a client; between 1994 and 2002, the U.S. Defense Department entered into over three thousand contracts, totaling an estimated $300 billion, with U.S.-based firms.[4]

This trend was then put on steroids after 9/11 and, more important, during the Iraq war, in which contractors substituted for a smaller than needed military force and the security situation involved multiple actors and no clear battle lines. During the first four years of the Iraq war, U.S. agencies awarded over $85 billion in contracts (almost 20% of the money appropriated by Congress for operations in Iraq) and hired approximately 190,000 contracted personnel.[5] To put this in perspective, the number of hired contractors was greater than the total amount of U.S. troops (roughly 170,000 at the height of the "surge") and by 2008 was roughly twenty-three times the number of allies' troops. The personnel in this "coalition of the billing" come from over thirty countries, with about a quarter American and the rest divided among third-country nationals and Iraqi citizens.

PMFs range from small consulting firms run by retired generals to transnational corporations leasing out fighter jets and skilled infantrymen. The industry can be divided into three basic business sectors:

1. Military provider firms, commonly known as private military companies (PMCs) or private security companies (PSCs), offer direct, tactical military assistance of an armed nature, including serving in combat. While humanitarian clients often prefer to work with "quiet" security providers like Olive, Hart, Armorgroup-DSL, and AKE, they have also hired firms with a wider media profile, such as Blackwater or Custer Battles.[6]

2. Military consulting firms draw on retired senior and non-commissioned officers to provide military advice and training but do not carry out operations. Relevant to the humanitarian sector, a wide range of companies provide training, threat assessment, security audits, and analysis to clients.[7] For example, after the 2003 bombing of the UN headquarters in Iraq, CARE hired former South African intelligence experts to help guide its safety concerns.[8]

3. Military support firms provide logistics, intelligence, and maintenance services. The biggest player in this sector is Halliburton and its KBR division, but other companies that have worked for humanitarian clients include DynCorp and PAE.[9] KBR's far-flung operations, for instance, have included helping to build and operate massive refugee camps during the Rwanda and Kosovo crises.

"DON'T ASK, DON'T TELL": HUMANITARIAN ACTORS AND PRIVATE MILITARY FIRMS

Just as the privatized military industry is diverse, so too is its clientele. It has ranged from "ruthless dictators, rebels, and drug cartels" to "legitimate sovereign states, respected multinational corporations, and humanitarian NGOs."[10] A somewhat surprising market niche is this latter humanitarian sector, especially given its claims to an ethic of neutrality and common practice of holding public military and peacekeeping forces at a distance (a source of great tension with U.S.-led coalition forces in places like Iraq and Afghanistan). Humanitarian actors make greater use of private military agents than is generally recognized; as one senior humanitarian security officer discussed, humanitarian actors use PMFs "more than people think," and this use "is growing."[11]

Typically, PMFs are hired in areas where the state government is unable to provide security and the international community is overextended or unwilling to dedicate sufficient resources. Unfortunately, these characteristics typify the very same environment in which humanitarians operate today.

In the redefinition of risk that is ongoing in the twenty-first century, humanitarians face what is increasingly viewed as the "double-edged sword of neutrality."[12] As a guiding principle, neutrality discourages self-armament and encourages holding armed factions, at a distance. At the same time, the conflicts that humanitarian agencies operate in increasingly feature local, nonprofessional, often criminal factions who often make no distinction between civilians and combatants in their violence. The result is that neutrality no longer guarantees protection for humanitarian actors, even creating a point of very active debate within the humanitarian field (for example, between the Red Cross and Doctors Without Borders) about whether the principle of "neutrality" has outlived its usefulness.

For example, between June 2006 and June 2007, there were 507 recorded cases of violent attack on UN personnel, 442 incidents of harassment and intimidation, 232 cases of physical assault, 126 cases of hijacking, and about 273 reported cases of arrest and detention by state and non-state actors. Data on non-UN agencies and organizations is patchy, but there is strong evidence that the security situation has grown worse over the last decade and particularly since 9/11 and the Iraq war. In 2003 alone, 76 humanitarian workers were killed by hostile action worldwide[13] (one U.S. government report on humanitarian work that year described it as "The Year of Living Dangerously"[14]). This sad growth in violence toward humanitarians continued through the decade, with 122 aid workers killed in 2008 and another 138 kidnapped or seriously injured in violent attacks.[15] As one human rights organization coordinator remarked, "There is no empirical evidence that declaring yourself to be neutral actually enhances your security."[16]

Though more and more armed crises demand a humanitarian presence, these situations are often too unsafe for aid agencies to operate without protection. At the same time, humanitarian actors typically under-invest in their own security. A 2004 survey of seventy-eight humanitarian organizations found systematic failures in the recruitment, training, and retention of qualified security managers due to a lack of funding and the absence of external pressure to manage security well.[17]

As more complex emergencies overwhelm the collective international capacity to respond effectively, the emerging private military marketplace has stepped forward to offer humanitarian organizations a means to enhance their capacities without turning to traditional state military assistance. In 2006, the Brookings Institution carried out a limited study on the issue that found more than forty contracts between PMFs and humanitarian actors in war zones, such as Afghanistan, Bosnia, the DRC, East Timor, Haiti, Iraq, Kosovo, Mozambique, Sierra Leone, Somalia, and Sudan.[18] These firms had gone to work for the full gamut of humanitarian actor types, including state agencies, international agencies, and both secular and religious, privately funded nongovernmental organizations (NGOs).

In 2008, the Humanitarian Policy Group followed up on Brookings' research with a global survey of aid organizations. As the subsequent report revealed, rather than being the anomaly once thought, "the contracting of certain security functions to external professionals has become increasingly common among humanitarian operations worldwide. This trend has followed both the rise in aid worker violence and the proliferation of international private security companies around the operations in Iraq and Afghanistan."[19]

The problem is that although the privatized military industry may open up possibilities, it also poses fundamental questions about the very future of the humanitarian ethic and identity.[20]

THE ROLE OF PMFS AND THE HUMANITARIAN RESPONSE

The situation in Iraq is an apt illustration of this massive change in public-private military relations as well as how the nature of contemporary conflict has stimulated humanitarian interest in investing in security and stability through PMFs. Government agencies, like the United States Agency for International Development (USAID) and the United Kingdom's Department for International Development (DFID), have engaged private military firms, as have non-governmental humanitarian organizations, like Save the Children and CARE.[21] The day-to-day movements and operations of these various PMFs are coordinated with a central operations center. This coordination center, the ROC (Regional Operations Center), is in turn contracted out to Aegis, a PMF. Notably, this firm is owned and operated by Tim Spicer, whose previous firm Sandline held controversial contracts in Africa and Papua New Guinea.[22] Aegis has also been investigated for insufficient screening and training of its employees and for a video released onto the Internet that showed its operators shooting at civilian vehicles, set to a rock song by Elvis Presley. The extent of how far things have changed in the humanitarian field is illustrated by one non-governmental humanitarian organization in the Brookings survey that had hired a PMF in Iraq to protect its facilities and staff; complete with its own sniper team.

Such contracts are more widespread than is publicly acknowledged. Koenraad Van Brabant, co-director of the Humanitarian Accountability Partnership International, noted that despite the common and growing use of PMFs, "there is widespread refusal to square up to the subject."[23] Most interviewees from the humanitarian community typically choose to stay anonymous, while representatives of the PMF community are often eager to discuss the topic but cite contract clauses that prevent them from full disclosure. Industry representatives in the 2006 survey estimated that approximately 25% of the "high-end" firms providing armed services and over 50% of firms providing logistical support have worked for humanitarian clients.[24] By comparison, interviews with humanitarian actors claim far lower figures. For example, one UN official stated that the entire organization had hired PMF personnel on only one occasion to do election monitoring.[25] However, the research for the 2006 study revealed that at least seven different UN agencies have hired PMFs for activities such as guarding UN personnel and offices in war zones and transporting food to refugees.

As the 2008 survey concluded, there is a huge disparity between public discussions of humanitarians' use of contracted security, most especially armed PMFs, and the reality. "No major humanitarian provider — UN, NGO or Red Cross — can claim that it has never paid for armed security. According to their headquarters respondents, over the past year at least 41% of the major humanitarian organizations contracted some form of armed protective services (guards, escorts or bodyguards) for one or more of their operations."[26]

There are several reasons why humanitarian groups and agencies downplay their links with PMFs. Doug Brooks, president of the International Peace Operations Association, a private military industry trade group, argues that it is simple pragmatism: "Too many NGOs would risk their funding bases if it were publicized that they were working with the peace and stability industry, no matter what the humanitarian benefits."[27] Robert Young Pelton, author of the book *Licensed to Kill: Hired Guns in the War on Terror*, puts it more bluntly: "They are of course hypocrites, because on one hand they say they don't want or need armed assistance, but as soon as they are kidnapped or blown up, they have two choices: Quit the area or hire muscle."[28]

Because humanitarian actors are in such denial, few are properly prepared for this type of contracting and thus deal with the industry from an ill-informed and unprepared position. The 2006 survey research found only three humanitarian agencies — Oxfam, Mercy Corps, and the International Committee of the Red Cross — that had formal documents on how their workers should relate to PMFs and their staff. A senior humanitarian security expert interviewed in 2006 knew of only one organization that had detailed oversight guidance for its contracted PMF employees, including rules of engagement, weapons handling procedures, and ammunition types. However, the organization had difficulty implementing the guidelines given the lack of expertise within its country teams.[29] Overall, the same conclusion was drawn when the issue was revisited at a global level two years later: "Guidance and procedures on whether, when and how to contract and manage private security companies, as a unique category of vendor requiring special criteria and oversight, are sorely lacking."[30]

How these issues can become quite complicated is illustrated by the case of one human rights organization that sent a reporting mission to Afghanistan. The team was recognized as a target for local insurgents but prevented by organizational rules and norms of neutrality from receiving any protection from the U.S.-led coalition forces. They were told by their headquarters to quietly hire armed security. Members of the team then flummoxed the senior staff back in New York; they asked what "rules of engagement" the NGO had decided upon as its organizational policy. There was, of course, no reply.[31]

Overall, interviews for the 2006 Brookings study revealed concern among humanitarian actors not only about issues of control over PMFs but also regarding access to simple information about the past activities of PMF personnel, pricing, and trends in the industry, all of which are needed simply to be smart clients.[32] There is no single place within either the international/UN system or the humanitarian research community where information on the connections and contracts between humanitarians and PMFs is gathered or processed. This means that current and future contracts are not informed by past lessons or systematically shared. In one blunt description by a refugee organization official, it was argued that humanitarian actors "don't have a clue" when it comes to hiring or managing military firms.[33]

PRIVATE MILITARY FIRMS AND HUMANITARIAN ACTION: POTENTIAL BENEFITS

A client hiring a private military firm does so with a number of rational and reasonable hopes. It hopes to gain the efficiency and expediency that often come from the business domain. PMFs can offer the potential of greater flexibility and agility than state or international organizations and can often call on more experienced and better-trained personnel than state or local forces. Thus, they may be able to operate more effectively and in fewer numbers on the ground while "outsourcing" the political consequences of soldiers being killed or wounded in action.

A key benefit to humanitarian actors pondering going down this route is that hiring PMFs regularizes and even professionalizes their security. Many humanitarian organizations already hire armed escorts or guards from local warlords. For instance, NGOs operating in Afghanistan, Chechnya/Ingushetia, the DRC, Yemen, and Somalia have had to develop quasi-contractual relationships with local "security" units or warlord groups. The 2008 study, for example, found that for any humanitarian group operating in south-central Somalia, "armed guards and escorts are omnipresent, and using them is widely viewed as the only possible way in which work can continue."[34] These relationships are often protection rackets in actuality, though; the guards are paid off mainly to prevent them or their affiliates from attacking an agency's assets or staff. If the choice is framed as between a khat-addled, teenaged gang member and a former Gurkha soldier, many humanitarians thus prefer the more professional alternative provided by PMFs.

Some argue that the role of PMFs could even go beyond the organizational client to include guarding local civilians, such as refugees. One firm, the International Executive Service Corps, has specifically targeted this sector in its marketing: "We strive to bring harmony and stability to regions under conflict, quickly and with the minimum of disruption to the local population. We are able to rapidly deploy, allowing stability to return, thus enabling deployment of aid. Agencies are then able to carry out emergency relief unhindered and without fear of physical harm."[35] According to the owner of Blackwater, another controversial firm that has aggressively marketed this side of its business potential, professional forces bypass the expense and diplomatic difficulties of "large-footprint" conventional forces.[36]

The most often cited case of privatization's promise in the humanitarian realm is the contrasting experiences in Sierra Leone of the firm Executive Outcomes and the UN's peacekeeping operation. In 1995, the government of Sierra Leone was near defeat by the Revolutionary United Front (RUF). The government hired the PMF Executive Outcomes, made up of veterans from the South African apartheid regime's elite forces, to help rescue it. Deploying a battalion-sized unit of assault infantry, combat helicopters, light artillery, and a few armored vehicles, Executive Outcomes was able within weeks to defeat the RUF and stabilize Sierra Leone for its first election in over a decade. After its contract's termination, however, war resumed. In 1999, the UN was sent in. But despite a budget and personnel size nearly twenty times those of the private firm, the UN force took several years of operations, and a rescue by the British military, to stabilize the environment enough for the next set of elections.[37]

Some argue, thus, that such private-sector activity opens up new possibilities for wholesale privatization of peacekeeping/enforcement operations. Personnel in the aforementioned South African firm Executive Outcomes performed a business exploration of its capacity to intervene in Rwanda in 1994. Internal plans claim that the company could have had armed troops on the ground within fourteen days and been fully deployed with over 1,500 of its own soldiers, along with air and fire support, within six weeks. The cost for a six-month operation to provide safe havens from the genocide was estimated at $150 million (around $600,000 a day). By comparison, the UN relief operation cost $3 million a day and came after the genocide.[38]

More recently, the idea has even been bandied about that firms could be hired to deploy to Darfur to fight off attacking militia, with many firms now including it in their business pitches and presentations to media and the public.[39] To serious analysts, however, the idea of out-sourcing such an operation is effectively a "non-starter" (to use the words of a UN official) as questions remain to be answered on everything from its funding and authorization to its actual makeup and just how it would keep from exacerbating the already complex political situation on the ground.[40] But the firms have gotten a great deal of PR mileage out of it (such as when actress/Darfur-activist Mia Farrow had a much publicized breakfast with Blackwater's owner), showing the strange new world we have entered in which for-profit military firms can posture to be more humanitarian in intent than the humanitarians themselves.

At a less controversial and more realistic level, humanitarian clients could clearly take better advantage of consulting and support firms. Con-sulting firms offer expertise in security assessments, analysis, and train-ing, key areas where humanitarian agencies are notably weak. The UN's Security in Iraq Accountability Panel found that for most organizations and agencies, security training, if given at all, consisted of providing humanitarian workers with an instructional CD-ROM on procedures. PMFs meanwhile could provide a detailed range of training,[41] as well as logistics, engineering, air transport, and other capacities that would greatly enhance aid distribution and provision.[42]

PRIVATE MILITARY FIRMS AND HUMANITARIAN ACTION: POTENTIAL PROBLEMS

There are, of course, many perils also involved in the use of private military firms, as the U.S. government has learned to its great dismay in recent years. While PMFs may offer the promise of operating more efficiently and effectively than public-sector forces, the reality has not always worked out that way. Instead, hiring private forces raises important concerns, including how contracts will be managed, contractual and control issues, legal accountability and liability matters, and long-term implications for the humanitarian community and the local political environment.

THE "CULTURE CLASH"

The first and perhaps most obvious source of tension is the possibility for misunderstanding resulting from the different backgrounds of private firms and humanitarian organizations. Firms come in with expectations shaped by their military backgrounds and often have trouble understanding not only individual NGOs but the humanitarian endeavor as a whole. Their staffs are not recruited, hired, or promoted with a humanitarian agenda in mind, nor are their operating procedures drawn from this field. Despite discussions for accommodating the practices of humanitarian clients, military firms in reality do typically impose their own business models, which reflect their own organizational DNA. As one humanitarian security officer put it bluntly, "They don't understand our community, period!... And in that lies a danger for our community."[43]

This, in turn, is reflected by the fact that many humanitarians look at PMFs the same way. Many find the military background and resulting organizational culture of many PMFs anathema or at the very least confusing.

MARKET REALITIES AND STAFFING ISSUES

The private military market is also quite fluid. If humanitarian clients don't have good screening, they end up with a mixed bag of PMF employees working on their behalf. In the early 1990s, when the industry started, the relatively limited number of PMFs allowed firms to choose the most qualified recruits and assemble teams who had worked together in units in the past and thus shared training and experience. The labor market, however, shifted away from such a structure during the Iraq boom. Few of the teams had ever worked together before, and at the high point of the boom, many firms found it difficult to find top personnel. One PMF employee, for instance, said that he had five competing contract offers (three in Iraq, one in Afghanistan, and one in Colombia).[44]

Like any other industry, these firms respond to changing markets by lowering hiring standards or sourcing new labor pools, such as bringing in third-party nationals. Indeed, contractors of more than thirty different nationalities have worked for PMFs in Iraq alone. This issue, though, creates not only new groups that have not worked together but also new issues of vetting to ensure proper skill sets.

The variability of the contractor labor market can also cover both skills and human rights concerns. PMF employees often represent elites within the military profession. There are many recently retired U.S. Special Forces operatives in Iraq, and more ex-Special Air Service (SAS) troops from the British Army work with PMFs in Iraq than serve in the current SAS force. However, firms have often oversold this. Many have also hired people with questionable experience or no military background at all. In Iraq, this problem has been magnified by the "gold rush effect" of new or rapidly expanding firms entering the market. With the rush for profits and the expanding need for personnel, many firms brought in less-skilled troops, including hiring those that had been cast off from other firms.[45]

Military firms also do not always look for the most congenial workforce, but instead recruit for effectiveness. It is completely understandable, but it can also yield results contrary to humanitarian ideals. For example, many former members of the most notorious and ruthless units of the Soviet and apartheid South Africa regimes have found employment in the private military industry, working for humanitarian clients in Sierra Leone, Liberia, Iraq, Sudan, and the DRC.[46] Even if it wanted to, for a firm to screen applicants can be difficult; few people list their human rights violations on their resume.

SCALING UP AND APPLICABILITY

Comparisons thus between imaginary PMF and real UN peacekeeping operations are often misleading. In the frequently cited example, Sierra Leone in 1995, few advocates mention that Executive Outcomes was contracted to push rebels back from the capital and secure diamond mines, not to handle the wider range of tasks demanded of a UN operation (election monitoring, demining, refugees, and so forth). It was also operating under different rules of engagement and political considerations. Executive Outcomes had a free rein to undertake any actions deemed necessary. UN peacekeepers, by comparison, are usually limited by rules of engagement that minimize their options on the use of force (there is debate over the definition of "self-defense," for example) and what constitutes permissible risk. Indeed, if hired by the UN or any other humanitarian client, a PMF would likely be comparatively hampered by similar challenges of mandate and procedural rules.

Peacekeeping differs markedly from military operations in its roles and responsibilities. It requires a culture and training focused on humanitarian concerns (particularly protecting civilians) that at times can conflict with standard military responses. Successful peacekeeping operations in Mozambique, Namibia, and Guatemala have included cease-fire monitoring, troop disarmament and demobilization, reconstruction, and election monitoring. Private military firms are typically ill equipped to handle these functions.

CONTRACTUAL ISSUES

The firms' aims of profit maximization are not always — and cannot always be — perfectly aligned with clients' interests. In any industry (and indeed even in nonprofits and such moral endeavors as humanitarian action), there always exist incentives to skirt corners, overcharge, pad personnel lists, hide failures, not perform to peak capacity, and so forth. While certainly not all PMFs act on such incentives (as, like firms in other industries, they refuse either out of honor or because they would be fearful of the consequences of getting caught), the private military market, like human nature, is not perfect, and some do.

Adding to this challenge, overseeing such contracts can be quite difficult, even for the largest clients. Indeed, one report on U.S. government contracting in the last five years identified 118 federal contracts, worth $745.5 billion, that had significant waste, fraud, abuse, or mismanagement, including several in the private military sector.[47] Thus, a humanitarian actor that opts to hire a firm must establish good policy and good business practices and hire sufficient staff to implement them. These include mechanisms for clear and competitive contract award processes emphasizing effectiveness and efficiency, oversight requirements to ensure compliance with contracts, and contingency plans for replacement in case of failure.

To properly manage PMF contracts, NGOs and humanitarian agencies will also need to develop what are unusual contract mechanisms and capabilities for a humanitarian, such as in-house military and security expertise. Hiring such firms requires knowledge of prevailing market rates for military functions and equipment and an ability to judge military skills, tactics, and rules of engagement. The problem is that no humanitarians have these capacities at present and developing such mechanisms demands a massive shift in humanitarian policy and guiding doctrines.

This question of management also entails a built-in irony. As the 2008 survey found, "One common concern was that the decision to contract out security services led to a tendency to externalise the organisation's security thinking, working against developing in-house capacities." That is, the motivating factor for hiring private security usually revolved around the lack of both personnel and intellectual capacity to do the job internally. But instead of addressing these problems, many outsourced. But this, in turn, brought in a slew of new personnel and management questions. So, the end result of the outsourcing "ironically also left organisations less able to manage their security providers in a responsible way."[48]

Privatization also raises certain problems of adverse selection, made worse by lessened accountability. There are no international controls governing whom PMFs work for. While a 2008 meeting in Montreux of legal representatives from seventeen states laid out a series of guidelines for firms and their government clients, two aspects stand out from their work: (1) their document, while laudable, was explicit that nothing in it was new or legally binding; and (2) the context of where these decisions are most often made is failed states, the exact place where such actors as the national signatories of the document are not operative or by any means fully in control.[49]

Firms make decisions based on assessments of business practices, domestic law, and perceived profitability. Just as the demand for PMF soldiers has risen as the conflicts in Iraq and Afghanistan have become more intense, the demand for such services will fall as the United States disengages militarily from the region. As the demand for their services in U.S.-directed operations lessens, there is a risk that PMFs will go "down market," so to speak. Because as a business, profit is the ultimate strategic motivator, firms or employees may become willing to work for clients and in locales that they would have refused to service previously while government money was coming in.

PMFs have worked for democracies, the UN, and humanitarian groups, but they have also worked for dictatorships, rebel groups, drug cartels, and pre-9/11, for two al-Qaeda-linked groups. The result is that a key issue for humanitarian actors is that they must account for concerns that the PMFs they hire are not involved in belligerent activities either in the same war zone or even elsewhere. (Such involvement will not only complicate the client's principles of neutrality but potentially implicate it in the eyes of local belligerents.) This is more easily said than done, though. The more successful the firm, the more likely that it has multiple clients. Also, many firms reflect the political priorities of their home state or even their individual executive. For instance, Blackwater's CEO, who proposed the hire of the firm to carry out UN peacekeeping, required his employees to take an oath of loyalty to the U.S. Constitution and issued a corporate newsletter celebrating President Bush's 2004 election win. This would make Blackwater attractive to some but unacceptable to others as a hire. Such firms may have not only multiple clients but even multiple personas. As the Blackwater firm developed a controversial public reputation from 2004 to 2008, it formed a network of as many as thirteen affiliate companies and ultimately renamed itself (to Xe), again illustrating the difficulties a client would have in keeping track of the whole and the raised internal costs it would take to do so effectively.

The reality is that a client only exerts an influence over a firm during its employment and only to the extent of their relative buying power. Clients must also be aware of the complexities of the firm's relationships and its shell structures and other hidden ownership. When the UN hired Lifeguard to guard its offices and personnel in Sierra Leone in 1999, the company was linked with Executive Outcomes, a firm that the UN had publicly excoriated in other environments.[50] A U.S. government agency similarly hired Aegis in Iraq without knowledge of the firm's controversial history.[51]

The kind of screening that hiring PMFs demands, difficult enough for governments, is beyond the capacity of humanitarian actors, who have rarely even tried to screen their firms in any formal manner.

There is no industry database, so humanitarian clients rely on "word of mouth," which has proven to be inadequate.[52] For example, Meteoric Tactical Solutions is a South Africa-based PMF (founded by ex–apartheid soldiers). In March 2004, two of its owners, including the firm's Iraq director, were arrested in Zimbabwe for being part of the alleged plot of an armed coup in Equatorial Guinea (they were accused of trying to purchase 61 AK-47 rifles; 45,000 rounds of ammunition; 1,000 rounds of anti-tank ammunition; and 160 grenades that would equip the coup force brought in by the Logo firm).[53] Other clients of the firm at the time included several humanitarian groups and the Swiss government.[54] Similar examples of humanitarian actors unwittingly (one hopes) hiring firms that have made questionable or embarrassing decisions include the U.K. Department for International Development and the demining charity Halo Trust hiring the air transport firm Aerocom (named by the UN for breaking international sanctions by transporting huge quantities of arms to Liberia) and the UN World Food Programme allegedly hiring air transport services from firms owned by the indicted international arms dealer Victor Bout, once dubbed the "merchant of death" by the British Foreign Minister.[55] In Uganda, the International Federation of Red Cross and Red Crescent Societies embarrassingly had to terminate a contract with a local company after it was discovered that the company was actually part of Saladin, a South African group linked with Executive Outcomes.[56]

QUESTIONS OF LAW, ACCOUNTABILITY, AND REGULATION

The global private military market is effectively unregulated. Although firms and their employees are bound by international humanitarian law (IHL), as all actors in war are, there remain significant uncertainties around their actual legal status and accountability. According to a senior official at a human rights organization, the "biggest concern is with the very gray place in the law when it comes to regulating these companies, especially in places like Iraq . . . Within this, where is the accountability for these firms? Who is holding them accountable? Who is checking up on them?"[57] These views were echoed by Human Rights Watch in the wake of the Abu Ghraib prison abuse scandal, noting with deep concern the "virtual immunity" of PMFs: "Allowing private contractors to operate in a legal vacuum is an invitation to abuse."[58] This lack of regulation can be as much of a problem for the military as for humanitarians. One senior U.S. military commander in Iraq reflected, "These guys run loose in this country and do stupid stuff. There's no authority over them, so you can't come down on them hard when they escalate force. They shoot people, and someone else has to deal with the aftermath."[59]

The only formal codes of conduct within the private military industry are voluntary ones that firms set for themselves, though there are attempts at wider self-regulation by trade groups. Member companies of one trade group, the International Peace Operations Association (IPOA), for example, have a code of conduct developed over several years that is commendable for its detail.[60] However, at the end of the day, it is a voluntary code, with no real teeth. It cannot impose any real sanctions to influence behavior, other than threats to expel a violating firm from a voluntary trade group. This was illustrated in 2007, after the shootings on September 16 in Bagdad's Nissor Square by members of the Blackwater company that left as many as seventeen Iraqi civilians dead. The IPOA announced it was exploring reviewing the firm, upon which Blackwater simply left the organization before the investigation could commence.[61] There were no fines, and the company lost no discernable contracts due to it no longer being in the trade group. Indeed, Blackwater simply then created its own organization, the humanitarian-appealingly named Peace and Stability Operations Institute.

In the legal sphere, it is often unclear which authority should investigate, prosecute, and punish crimes committed by PMFs and/or their employees. This leaves a legal near-vacuum where it is unclear how business organizations and corporate chains of command are held accountable for war crimes; according to one military law analyst, "legally speaking, they [military contractors] fall into the same grey area as the unlawful combatants detained at Guantanamo Bay."[62]

The military has an established court-martial system to which soldiers are accountable wherever they are located. Since 2007, contractors working on behalf of the U.S. military in a contingency operation could potentially fall under the Uniform Code of Military Law, the same system of law that public soldiers fall under. Yet, the applicability of this law to private soldiers remains untested legally. (Only one case has been utilized, and it did not involve a U.S. citizen nor go to trial, with the accused, an Iraqi contractor accused of stabbing a fellow Iraqi contractor during an argument, accepting a plea bargain.) It is questionable whether it would be applied to those working on humanitarian agency operations, even in such contingency zones.

Like other actors, PMFs are supposed to be bound by international laws. But international law still lacks a means of enforcement. The obligation to enforce rests with local states. But PMFs, like humanitarian organizations, typically operate in fragile or failed states; indeed, the absence of an effective local state is usually the cause for their presence.

If the local state is lacking, true legal enforcement is left then to emanate from the home state(s) of the firm and the client, but such extraterritorial attempts to exercise legal powers across borders are not only incredibly difficult in practice but also raise problems of sovereignty. The few states with effective laws lack means to enforce them abroad, as was the case in the failed attempts by South Africa and Nepal to prevent their citizens from working for PMFs in Iraq. The humanitarians that hired these troops were aiding and abetting something that was illegal, but unenforceable, back home. Many PMFs, meanwhile, register in locales like the Caymans or the Channel Isles and operate though subsidiaries registered elsewhere to evade legislation and taxes in their home states.

In the United States, the primary vector for such legal investigation and enforcement on the civilian side is the Military Extraterritorial Jurisdiction Act (MEJA). It, however, just covers contractors working in support of the mission of the Department of Defense who have committed a felony while abroad. How far this extends is open to interpretation, meaning that it still remains unclear, for example, whether the Blackwater employees at Nissor Square (under a State Department contract, but in an active war zone) fall under MEJA or not. For a contractor employed by a humanitarian NGO, the application of MEJA would be very difficult to envision. Moreover, using MEJA has proven so far to be more theory than practice, as the ability of a civilian prosecutor to successfully investigate and prosecute crimes in a war zone thousands of miles away so far has been limited. Indeed, out of the more than 190,000 contractors in Iraq, only two MEJA cases have been brought so far, one for possession of child pornography and one for assault on a fellow contractor. Neither involved potential crimes against local civilians and neither contractor was working for a humanitarian agency.

Law is not only about criminal consequences for individual perpetrators. Humanitarian actors must also address questions of organizational responsibility. Just as states cannot release themselves from their obligations under international humanitarian law by hiring PMFs to do their work for them, neither can humanitarian clients. Thus, violations by a firm hired without proper guidance, management, and screening could leave the humanitarian client culpable. The U.S. government, for example, faces issues of accountability surrounding civilian deaths attributed to its hired contractors in Iraq.[63] It is for this reason that many in the Congress and military are pushing for PMFs, as a condition of their contract profits, to be brought under the authority of the military law system, which would set up a systematic mechanism for providing accountability in a war zone. How this might carry over to humanitarian clients is an issue rich for debate.

But accountability should not merely be framed as a legal issue, nor even one for the very contractors themselves. That is, the question of client accountability when PMFs are hired is fascinating because it brings to the fore a question that surrounds the broader humanitarian community—to whom are humanitarians ultimately accountable? Their donors? Their constituents? And just who are these donors or constituents, and on what basis are they so empowered versus other possible authorities?

Ambiguity also surrounds questions of not merely accountability but also liability in conflict zones (as an aside, there is also dispute over what defines such a zone; much like a "failed state," it is often open to wide interpretation). The private military industry is a new industry, and cases in civil courts are just now beginning to establish its legal structures. Currently, Iraqi torture victims are suing CACI International for its employees' role as interrogators at Abu Ghraib, accusing them, among other things, of violating the Racketeer Influenced and Corrupt Organizations Act (RICO). Families of Blackwater employees killed at Fallujah have sued the firm for allegedly breaking its contract when it deployed forces with less training and equipment and in fewer numbers than previously planned.[64] Humanitarian organizations hiring PMFs thus must weigh whether these questions of culpability and liability will affect them in the civil court system, but also how such lawsuits will affect them in the court of public opinion and in the eyes of donors.

The humanitarian crisis that occurred after Hurricane Katrina demonstrated that this issue is not one that takes place only outside the United States and in the developing world. There is also a brewing demand for PMFs to be involved in domestic emergency response. After the systemic failure in the hurricane's wake, Blackwater and an Israeli private security company were deployed by private citizens and companies in the failed state that was New Orleans. After being hired to provide security and evacuation services to private clients, these and other private military operators were then contracted by public authorities into much more diverse roles. Blackwater, for instance, was given a $42 million contract with the Department of Homeland Security to provide security to FEMA sites. These included dispute resolution centers, where Katrina refugees (American citizens) often became angry and threatened the FEMA workers. Similarly, the St. Bernard Parish sheriff's office contracted with DynCorp to provide one hundred employees to be deputized. This allowed the private military contractors to make arrests, carry weapons, and wear St. Bernard Parish sheriff's office uniforms. The goal was that "you wouldn't be able to tell the difference" between the regular force and the DynCorp employees.[65]

As planning continues for what to do in future crises like Katrina, it is clear some are contemplating the use of such firms within the nation's borders. In 2006, KBR reportedly received from the Department of Homeland Security a $385 million contingency contract. It entailed that the firm be on call to build large base camps inside the United States (much like it did in the Balkans and Iraq LOGCAP [Logistics Civil Augmentation Program] contracts) as well as "temporary detention and processing capabilities" able to hold up to 5,000-plus detainees.[66]

Such government contracts raise a number of legal and ethical issues, especially when dealing with militarized security against American citizens. Disparity in pay between contractors and locals has the potential to cause tension within public safety forces and could undermine efforts to ultimately rebuild what is essentially a public institution. These contracts also bring to light the overarching question of which government functions should inherently require public servants to perform them.

But there is also a broader issue: When is it okay or not for a humanitarian organization, a hotel CEO, a wealthy landowner, or any other private citizen inside the United States to hire their own private military? And who decides when this right kicks in?

In essence, what we should be asking at a deeper level is how far are we internally willing to tolerate a system that affords protection only to those with sufficient levels of wealth? This is not just a theoretic matter. For example, Sovereign Deed was a company founded by former executives of Triple Canopy, a private military firm active in Iraq. The firm's whole business plan was devoted to providing armed teams that would carry out personal rescue and evacuation services for wealthy individuals in areas affected by natural or man-made disasters. Described as an "insurance policy" for the hyper-rich, Sovereign Deed clients were to pay a flat fee of $50,000 to join and $15,000 upwards in periodic fees thereafter. It was a tiered service; those clients who paid the most would have the greatest chances of survival.[67]

What such services entail is the provision of force parallel to what occurred in the 2007 wildfires in California. While public forces were overwhelmed by the sheer expanse of the fires, private firefighting teams deployed, but only to help the people who paid $19,000 in annual premiums to insurance giant American International Group (AIG, the very same company later bailed out by the American public). Their homes were preventatively sprayed with a special fire retardant and further protected by private fire trucks that skirted through police blockades to service client homes in need. The result was a structure that saved people's homes based not on who was most in danger but rather on who paid AIG. As one firefighter working on contract for AIG told Bloomberg News, "There were a few instances where we were spraying and the neighbor's house went up like a candle."[68]

The rich have always had access to better goods and services, but it is worth questioning whether this should also apply to basic issues of survival in a time of disaster, massive terror attack, or worse. As Dr. Irwin Redlener of Columbia University puts it, "In the face of a major calamity, everyone else is screwed. It doesn't sound American."[69]

ISSUES FOR THE LONG TERM

Privatization offers many seeming advantages and capabilities that a humanitarian organization would be hard pressed to realize on its own.

But we must recognize that a private military company can provide only what it is paid to do. It is a temporary mechanism for creating a bubble around humanitarians in a dangerous situation or accessing military-like capacities in training or logistics. It cannot, however, address the underlying causes of unrest and violence. Many humanitarian employees also worry that the presence of PMFs compromises local perceptions of aid groups' neutrality and increases the number of armed forces present in a conflict zone, potentially even exacerbating an already complex situation. U.S. military officers came to a similar conclusion, noting that the gains in manpower made by hiring PMFs were often undermined by the negative effect on counterinsurgency efforts.[70]

There is also the issue of displacement of threat. While PMFs protect their clients—aid workers and aid facilities—other unprotected local groups, such as the poor or refugees, may face increased risks. Some might argue that the privatization of security will free up public forces to better protect the rest of society. But in practice, the worst threats are deflected from privately protected areas, and the rest of society must rely on declining, unstable, or nonexistent public means.

More broadly, the privatization of security risks reinforces internal "have and have not" divisions in weak states between those who enjoy security and those who do not. When security is a profit-driven exercise, the wealthy are inherently favored. The incorporation of this mentality into the humanitarian sector is not a happy development as it certainly does not meld with humanitarian ideals. Moreover, determining who enjoys protection and who does not is a political act; when they hire PMFs, humanitarian actors are taking upon themselves decisions that were once the prerogative of the state.

In weighing these issues, such outside forces should also ensure to never forget the tension that is always present in humanitarian ventures: that the risk taken by those intervening is never equal to the risk borne by those needing intervention/aid. Despite the humanitarian creed that all lives are equal, the cold reality is that the relationship of outside humanitarians to those locals in need is already privileged. One side can choose when and where to intervene and, now, whether to bring in its own protection. Those "aided" do not have such choices.

CONCLUSIONS: THINK FIRST, PRIVATIZE BETTER

The confluence of the private military industry and the humanitarian community raises a series of tough questions that must be openly faced rather than kept quiet. As one senior human rights official explained, "Before we contract out [with such firms], we need to be unbelievably careful to work out the full implications."[71] The dimensions of this complex issue range from carefully considering potential scenarios to weighing the political, legal, ethical, and reputational ramifications. This is crucial, as the one non-negotiable rule of hiring PMFs is that humanitarians have a firm "responsibility to prevent and mitigate any possible negative outcomes."[72]

The very first step in this effort must be to get past a psychological defense mechanism that the community seems to be running up against, one first postulated by Sigmund Freud, in which a person is faced with a fact that is too uncomfortable to accept. Or, as the television personality "Dr. Phil" might diagnose the humanitarian world: "If you're in denial about it, if you're minimizing it, if you're trivializing it, if you're conning yourself about it, then you'll never get where you need to be."[73]

What was once "abnormal" has become the new normal when it comes to PMFs and humanitarians. Thus, humanitarians must strive to develop the working norms and protocols that can best guide and regulate these challenging interventions. The current situation is particularly exacerbated by the twin "information deficits" that surround this issue: first, a "lack of transparent information" on the private military industry itself and its contracts with humanitarians, and second, humanitarians' "reluctance to share with others what knowledge and experience they do possess."[74] One step would be for the major agencies and groups to agree to undertake a full accounting of their contacts and contracts with PMFs and move past their present state of denial toward the extent of humanitarian-PMF relations. Such accounting will generate a body of data for lessons learned about best practices and the vetting of firms. In their advocacy efforts, humanitarian groups should also support current government efforts to assemble data on the extent, type, and contract performance of PMFs hired by the public sector, to increase marketplace transparency for all parties.

Indeed, because of the various displacement effects discussed above, it can be argued that this sort of action is a moral responsibility of each organization toward the community as a whole. As the 2008 survey of humanitarian groups found, "One organisation's security stance inevitably affects the others around it; its sharing (or otherwise) of security information has knock-on effects for the entire community. Yet thus far, only very limited discussion has taken place at the interagency level on the use of private security providers."[75] Models for how to initiate this effort include pulling lessons from country-specific NGO coordinating councils, such as the NGO Coordination Committee in Iraq, which created a common forum for in-country humanitarian groups to share information on a variety of issues and build toward a common platform for operational decisionmaking.

The humanitarian community must also determine when and where it is appropriate to hire PMFs (and thus in turn, when it is not), who should hire them (and who should not), how to interact with them in the field, and what rights and responsibilities the community has toward PMF employees (including as detainees and prisoners). That is, if the decision is made to go down this privatization pathway, agencies should be more judicious when contracting with these firms. They should weigh fully long- and short-term benefits and should constantly update their analyses based on developing local public capacities. They must ensure that contracting is carried out in accordance with, and supported by, the appropriate political authorities. If humanitarian agencies continue to expand their use of PMFs, they will require internal institutional changes. Agencies will need to amend their oversight processes and hire new staff to oversee contracts and may also need to recruit their own in-house military expertise.[76]

For the broader humanitarian community, a good starting point for change would be the creation of standardized monitoring and contracting processes. Priorities would include the establishment of clear contractual standards and incentives programs, the creation of systems for the outside vetting of personnel, and the formation of teams of independent observers with the powers to monitor and control payments in order to establish their authority over a firm. The UN and/or umbrella aid organizations might establish a database of vetted and financially transparent firms that have met international standards, to be constantly updated by independent military observers and auditors hired to monitor contracts. The humanitarian community must also consider rules of engagement by which forces contracted by humanitarians should operate, limitations on weaponry, and guidelines for whether forces should be identified as armed, but civilian, combatants. Finally, the humanitarian community must discuss whether measures are needed to distinguish humanitarian vehicles and personnel from PMF ones amid the proliferation of civilian actors—and their often interchangeable SUVs—in combat zones.

Humanitarian actors should explore ways to enhance their control of contracted PMFs. Possibilities include exclusivity clauses to avoid firms double-billing for assets shared across contracts, collective action in contracting to enhance buying power and market clout, and collaboration with insurance firms (who often contract with both humanitarian clients and PMFs) to set and maintain standards for vetting.

The most important step would be to bring PMFs under the control of the law. Such a clarification and expansion of both international and national law (including bringing contractors under the universal code of military justice) is certainly not within the power of humanitarian actors, but they can and should lobby for it. Individual agencies could include clauses in contracts specifying training requirements for PMF employees in both technical practice and IHL. Contracts could also provide for enhanced monitoring by third parties, establish performance benchmarks, mandate evaluations, and require accreditation. Agencies could also incorporate "whistleblower" protections and the rights of third parties (including local beneficiaries) to enforce contractual terms through lawsuits.[77]

In all these areas, there will likely be unwillingness of individual humanitarian actors or the broader community as a whole to act. For this reason, greater incentives will have to be established. For instance, the major aid donors should seek to enhance their influence in this area, such as by establishing among them common principles of security funding.[78] Indeed, at the end of the day, it is their money that is being spent on such contracts.

If any of these steps seem daunting or too problematic, there is a simple answer: don't go down this pathway. That is, the step of hiring private military firms is an important one that should be weighed with due consideration, especially in humanitarian endeavors. If it is not, then success will likely not be had.

In an ideal world, humanitarian action would be left to humanitarian actors. In reality, PMFs are already in contact with or working for humanitarian actors in almost every war zone. Though it may have Henry Dunant (the founder of the Red Cross) spinning in his grave, such a confluence of military, business, and humanitarian interests constitutes a defining change in the twenty-first century humanitarian landscape — and one that must be forthrightly faced.

NOTES

1. While the term privatized military firm (PMF) is used here to denote the wide range of military roles that make up the private military industry, many use the term private military company (PMC) or private security company (PSC). Yet technically, PMC or PSC denote only the armed sector of firms providing tactical services.

2. For more on the history of the private military industry, see P. W. Singer, *Corporate Warriors: The Rise of the Privatized Military Industry* (Ithaca, NY: Cornell University Press, 2003), 19–39.

3. U.S. Agency for International Development (USAID), "Contracts and Grants," Assistance for Iraq, www.usaid.gov/iraq/activities.html. In a similar way, there has been an increasing tendency to outsource functions to the non-governmental aid sector. Roughly 75% of USAID's activities are carried out by a mix of for-profit companies and not-for-profit NGOs. In Iraq, USAID has contracted work worth more than $3.2 billion to for-profit firms.

4. Phillip van Niekerk, "Making a Killing: The Business of War," Center for Public Integrity, International Consortium of Investigative Journalists, October 28, 2002, http://projects.publicintegrity.org/bow/report.aspx?aid=147.

5. Congressional Budget Office, *Contractors' Support of U.S. Operations in Iraq* (Washington, DC, August 2008), 1.

6. Author interview with industry expert, September 2005; and Robert Young Pelton, e-mail message to author, September 19, 2005.

7. Koenraad Van Brabant, "Humanitarian Action and Private Security Companies," *Humanitarian Exchange* 20 (March 2002).

8. Robert Young Pelton, e-mail message to author, September 19, 2005.

9. Author interview with industry executive, September 2005.

10. Doug Brooks and Hussein Solomon, "From the Editor's Desk," *Conflict Trends*, 2000, no. 1 (June).

11. Author interview with senior humanitarian security officer, September 28, 2005.

12. Author interview with humanitarian security officer, September 24, 2005.

13. UN General Assembly, Sixty-second Session, Report of the Secretary-General, *Safety and Security of Humanitarian Personnel and Protection of UN Personnel,*

A/62/324, October 5, 2007; Roberta Cohen, "Safety for Those Who Bring Help," Washington Post, November 3, 2003; and UN News Service, "Secretary General Reports High Number of Attacks on UN Staff Overseas," October 10, 2003.

14 D. King, "The Year of Living Dangerously: Attacks on Humanitarian Aid Workers in 2003," US Department of State, 2004.

15 Abby Stoddard, Adele Harmer, and Victoria DiDomenico, "Providing Aid in Insecure Environments: 2009 Update," HPG Policy Brief 34 (London: Humanitarian Policy Group, April 2009), http://www.cic.nyu.edu/Lead%20Page%20PDF/HPG_2009%20.pdf.

16 Author interview, September 2005.

17 European Commission Humanitarian Aid Department, *Report on Security of Humanitarian Personnel: Standards and Practices for the Security and Advocacy for Humanitarian Space* (Brussels: ECHO, 2004).

18 P. W. Singer, "Humanitarian Principals, Private Military Agents: Some Implications of the Privatized Military Industry for the Humanitarian Community," in *Resetting the Rules of Engagement: Trends and Issues in Military–Humanitarian Relations*, Humanitarian Policy Group Report 22, ed. Victoria Wheeler and Adele Harmer (Washington, DC: Brookings Institute, 2006), http://www.brookings.edu/articles/2006/02defenseindustry_singer.aspx.

19 Abby Stoddard, Adele Harmer, and Victoria DiDomenico, "Private Security Contracting in Humanitarian Operations," HPG Policy Brief 33 (London: Humanitarian Policy Group, January 2009), http://www.odi.org.uk/resources/download/2844.pdf.

20 Complications emerge sometimes in quite unexpected areas. For example, discussions in the U.S. Congress in April 2005 explored having USAID determine what type of military equipment and training private soldiers in Iraq should have and then regulate its use.

21 DFID, for example, employs Control Risks Group to provide armed protection for its staff and to give intelligence and security advice. DFID, "Memorandum Submitted by the Department for International Development," October 2004; and Tony Vaux et al., *Humanitarian Action and Private Security Companies: Opening the Debate* (London: International Alert, 2001), http://www.reliefweb.int/rw/lib.nsf/db900SID/LGEL-5F9JNU/$FILE/intalert-security.pdf?OpenElement.

22 Mary Pat Flaherty, "Iraq Work Awarded to Veteran of Civil Wars," *Washington Post*, June 16, 2004; see also P. W. Singer, "Nation Builders and Low Bidders in Iraq," *New York Times*, June 15, 2004.

23 Van Brabant, "Humanitarian Action."

24 Author interview with industry representatives, September 2005.

25 Author interview with UN official, September 2005.

26 Stoddard, Harmer, and DiDomenico, "Private Security Contracting."

27 Doug Brooks, e-mail message to author, August 28, 2005.

28 Robert Young Pelton, e-mail message to author, September 19, 2005.

29 Author interview with senior humanitarian security expert, September 29, 2005.

30 Stoddard, Harmer, and DiDomenico, "Private Security Contracting."

31 Author interview with human rights organization coordinator, September 2005.

32 Author interviews with humanitarian officials, July 2005.

33 Author interview with refugee organization official, September 2005.

34 Stoddard, Harmer, and DiDomenico, "Private Security Contracting."

35 Cited in Daniel Hellinger, "Humanitarian Action, NGOs and the Privatization of the Military," *Refugee Survey Quarterly* 23, no. 4 (2004): 192–220.

36 Eric Prince, statement made at the 16th Annual National Defense Industrial Association Special Operations and Low-Intensity Conflict symposium, February 2005.

37 Doug Brooks, "Messiahs or Mercenaries? The Future of International Private Military Services," *International Peacekeeping* 7, no. 4 (2000): 129–44; and Doug Brooks, "Write a Cheque, End a War: Using Private Military Companies to End African Conflicts," *Conflict Trends*, 2000, no. 1 (June).

38 For more on this episode, please see Singer, *Corporate Warriors*, chap. 11.

39 Max Boot, "Send in the Mercenaries," *Los Angeles Times*, May 31, 2006; and Frank Langfitt, "Private Military Firm Pitches Its Services in Darfur," NPR, All Things Considered, May 26, 2006, http://www.npr.org/templates/story/story.php?storyId=5433902.

40 Traci Hukill, "Should Peacekeepers Be Privatized?" *National Journal*, May 19, 2004. Also available at http://www.progress.org/2004/merco1.htm under the title "Lobbying for Mercenaries: Selling Mercenaries to the U.N. as 'Privatized Peacekeeping.'"

41 Hellinger, "Humanitarian Action, NGOs."

42 Peter H. Gantz, "The Private Sector's Role in Peacekeeping and Peace Enforcement," Global Policy Forum, November 18, 2003.

43 Author interview with senior humanitarian expert, September 29, 2005.

44 Author interview with privatized military firm employee, Washington, DC, September 2004.

45 For more on this, see Robert Young Pelton, *Licensed to Kill* (New York: Crown, 2006).

46 Singer, *Corporate Warriors*, chap. 7, 11, and 14.

47 House Committee on Government Reform, Special Investigations Division, Dollars Not Sense: Contracting Under the Bush Administration," June 2006, http://oversight.house.gov/documents/20061211100757-98364.pdf.

48 Stoddard, Harmer, and DiDomenico, "Private Security Contracting."

49 Swiss Federal Department of Foreign Affairs, "Montreux Document on Private Military and Security Companies (PMSCs)," media release, September 17, 2008, http://www.eda.admin.ch/eda/en/home/recent/media/single.html?id=21497.

50 Jack Kelly, "Safety at a Price," *Pittsburgh Post Gazette*, February 13, 2000.

51 Singer, "Nation Builders and Low Bidders."

52 Author interview with humanitarian organization official, September 29, 2005.

53 Antony Barnett, Solomon Hughes, and Jason Burke, "Mercenaries in 'Coup Plot' Guarded UK officials in Iraq," *Guardian*, June 6, 2004.

54 Barnett, Hughes, and Burke, "Mercenaries."

55 Barnett, Hughes, and Burke, "Mercenaries"; and author interview with PMF industry expert, September 2005. Other clients of the Bout network of firms have included Halliburton. Michael Isikoff, "Iraq: Government Deal With a 'Merchant of Death'?" *Newsweek*, December 20, 2004.

56 Vaux et al., *Humanitarian Action*, 17.

57 Author interview with senior official at a human rights organization, October 11, 2005.

58 Human Rights Watch, "Iraq: U.S. Prisoner Abuse Sparks Concerns Over War Crimes," *Human Rights Watch News*, April 30, 2004, http://www.hrw.org/english/docs/2004/04/30/iraq8521.htm.

59 Jonathan Finer, "Security Contractors in Iraq Under Scrutiny After Shootings," *Washington Post*, September 10, 2005.

60 International Peace Operations Association, Code of Conduct 11 (Washington, DC: IPOA, December 1, 2006), http://ipoaworld.org/eng/codeofconduct/91-codecode ofconductv11eng.html.

61 International Peace Operations Association, "IPOA Statement Regarding the Membership Status of Blackwater USA," press release, October 12, 2007, http://community.icontact.com/p/ipoaonline/newsletters/press/posts/ipoa-statement-regarding-the-membership-status-of-blackwater-usa.

62 Singer, "Nation Builders and Low Bidders."

63 Among these incidents were ones in which the providers were protecting clients on humanitarian missions, such as a shooting in Irbil, which allegedly involved a DynCorp team guarding a USAID convoy. Finer, "Security Contractors in Iraq."

64 Emad Mekay, "Torture Victims Sue U.S. Security Companies," Inter Press Service, June 10, 2004.

65 Renae Merle, "Storm-Wracked Parish Considers Hired Guns: Contractors in Louisiana Would Make Arrests, Carry Weapons," *Washington Post*, March 14, 2006.

66 Peter Dale Scott, "Homeland Security Contracts for Vast New Detention Camps," New America Media, January 31, 2006. See also Katherine Hunt, "KBR Awarded Homeland Security Contract Worth Up To $385M," Marketwatch, January 24, 2006, http://www.marketwatch.com/story/kbr-awarded-homeland-security-contract-worth-up-to-385m.

67 Anne Stanton, "Is Survival Only for The Rich?" *Northern Express*, December 13, 2007, http://www.northernexpress.com/editorial/features.asp?id=2869 .

68 Daniel Taub, "AIG's Fire Trucks Save Homes of Wealthy Californians," Bloomberg News Service, October 26, 2007, http://www.bloomberg.com/apps/news?pid=20601087&sid=af3wCbWHvK4w&refer=home.

69 Stanton, "Is Survival Only."

70 Jeffrey S. Thurnher, "Drowning in Blackwater: How Weak Accountability over Private Security Contractors Significantly Undermines Counterinsurgency Efforts," *Army Lawyer*, July 1, 2008, https://www.jagcnet.army.mil/JAGCNETInternet/Homepages/AC/ArmyLawyer.nsf/c82df279f9445da185256e5b005244ee/53e4adaced233926852574b30056099f/$FILE/Article%205%20-%20By%20MAJ%20Jeffrey%20S.%20Thurnher.pdf.

71 Author interview with senior official at a human rights organization, October 11, 2005.

72 Stoddard, Harmer, and DiDomenico, "Private Security Contracting."

73 Phil McGraw, "Seven Steps to Breaking Your Addiction," Dr. Phil, http://www.drphil.com/articles/article/173.

74 Stoddard, Harmer, and DiDomenico, "Private Security Contracting."

75 Stoddard, Harmer, and DiDomenico, "Private Security Contracting."

76 USAID had only three personnel on the ground in Iraq to oversee three billion dollars worth of contracts in 2003. The agency sought to solve the problem by contracting out oversight. The overall number of U.S. Defense Department contract officers has fallen by roughly 50%, while the amount of contracting increased by 12% a year between 1990 and 2000. See U.S. Comptroller General, "March 19 Hearing on Sourcing and Acquisition—Questions for the Record," GAO-03-771R (Washington, DC, May 23, 2003); Laura Dickinson, "Public Law Values in a Privatized World" (paper presented at The Future of the State Conference, University of Virginia, October 8, 2005); and Shane Harris, "AID Plans to Contract Out Oversight of Iraq Contracts," Government Executive.com, May 20, 2003, http://www.govexec.com/story_page.cfm?filepath=/dailyfed/0503/052003h1.htm.

77 Dickinson, "Public Law Values."

78 Stoddard, Harmer, and DiDomenico, "Private Security Contracting."

CHAPTER FOUR

Risking Health | *HIV/AIDS and the Problem of Access to Essential Medicines*

HEINZ KLUG

After twenty years, the human immunodeficiency virus/acquired immune deficiency syndrome (HIV/AIDS) pandemic has finally been recognized as a global health crisis, yet the debate over access to the public goods that are essential to defeating this scourge—antiretroviral medicines (ARVs)—continues to be shaped less by principles of public health than by concerns over unrestricted trade and intellectual property rights. This is so despite a general understanding that the HIV/AIDS pandemic is the "defining humanitarian catastrophe of our time"[1] and that it is the availability of antiretroviral drugs that shapes the impact this pandemic is having on different societies. Availability of these medicines has transformed the pandemic in developed countries into a chronic manageable disease, while in developing countries over three million people continue to suffer AIDS-related deaths every year. Sustainable access to affordable medicines is thus central to any strategy to address this pandemic. After over twenty million deaths the question of AIDS is no longer purely a problem of medical science but increasingly a question of social, political, and legal equity—a question of where the risk of a global health crisis should fall: on the individuals who become infected, the societies that bear the burden of high rates of infection, or the international community and global pharmaceutical corporations that now have the scientific capacity to address this catastrophe?

In developing countries in particular, the ability of governments to effectively combat the pandemic is dependent on a variety of issues; however, the question of access to medicines remains of central concern. As in the case of other diseases, the availability of pharmaceuticals is only one aspect of a comprehensive health system needed in any country, but it is an element that grew in significance as well as cost over the course of the twentieth century. Advances in the understanding of diseases, the biological sciences, and chemistry produced three distinct pharmaceutical revolutions—resulting in sulphonamide, penicillin, and cortisone medicines—during this period.[2] These breakthroughs have transformed the field of medical practice so that modern pharmaceuticals now play a central part in addressing humanity's disease burdens. While preventive medicine and access to clean water might still guarantee the greatest and most cost-effective public health benefits, access to essential medicines has become an integral element of public health strategies around the globe.

With an estimated 33.2 million HIV-positive people in the world,[3] the pandemic poses a potentially destabilizing threat to both individual communities and society more generally. Yet the existence of a medical regime that allows HIV-positive individuals to live extended and productive lives has potentially transformed the very nature of this pandemic. It is this transformation that has generated a transnational social movement and raised important questions about the relationship between domestic demands for social and economic justice and international claims of property rights and economic freedom.[4] While patents are not the sole reason why developing countries have failed to adequately respond to the pandemic, it is only access to antiretroviral medicines that will enable countries to respond to this crisis in an effective way. Increasingly there is acknowledgment of a close relationship between prevention and treatment strategies, including the possibility that the drugs may not only suppress the effects of the virus but may also reduce the incidence of transmission. The availability of ARVs enhances efforts to encourage people to engage in voluntary testing and preventive behaviors. It is the combination of a viable medicines regime linked to testing and preventive education that provides the greatest opportunity to undermine the social stigma and denial that are fueling this pandemic.

In developing countries that have not had the capacity—in production, budget, or political will—to effectively address the HIV/AIDS pandemic, the outcome is a continuing disaster. Even as it has slipped from the news cycle, the effect of the pandemic on health systems, families, and communities amounts to an ongoing process of degradation. As the pandemic has taken on a social profile that disproportionately affects the poor and marginalized, so has the provision of a limited supply of medicines through philanthropic efforts and some public facilities pushed the pandemic into the background. The only truly successful response in a developing country has been the example of Brazil, where the government early on adopted innovative programs to provide access to the newly available antiretroviral medications. Brazil has also used its production capacity to produce medicines and where necessary threaten the pharmaceutical corporations that it would issue compulsory licenses if they refused to provide the necessary medicines to the state at reasonable prices. The failure or inability of most developing countries, particularly in Africa, to follow what the World Health Organization has described as Brazil's best practices model means that the risk posed by the continuing HIV/AIDS pandemic continues to be "privatized" as it is borne by individuals, families, and communities without the effective intervention of a global, public health–driven response.

Access to medicines is, however, not only a question of public health. In developing countries in particular the question of access to medicines has become part of the broader debate over trade and the ongoing struggle over intellectual property rights in the global economy. To understand why the pharmaceutical industry played such a major role in promoting the globalization of intellectual property rights and the international Agreement on Trade-Related Aspects of Intellectual Property Rights (TRIPS), it is necessary to recognize the structural conditions implicit in the production of pharmaceuticals that drive this goal. Research-oriented pharmaceutical manufacturers argue that they are involved in a risky business, in which on average only one "commercially viable drug emerges from every 4,000 to 10,000 compounds screened in a development process that may involve ten years of testing and clinical trials for efficacy and safety."[5] Compounding the high costs of development, however, are the relatively low costs of product imitation—through reverse engineering—and production, creating what economists refer to as the appropriability problem. Patent law, which aims to reward innovation by providing a limited monopoly to the patent holder, provides one means for intellectual property–intensive industries, such as the pharmaceutical industry, to pursue profitability. While the industry emphasizes the importance of patent protection, particularly product patents, it is important to recognize that there exist a range of strategies and opportunities through which the major multinational pharmaceutical companies have until now competed successfully—even in jurisdictions in which there has been no intellectual property protection at all.

But medical innovation is not simply a question of profitability. The World Health Organization (WHO) points out that medicines are "not simply just another commodity" but rather a public good.[6] Access to essential drugs, from this perspective, is a critical part of the fundamental human right to health.[7] According to Dr. Michael Scholtz, WHO's executive director of health technology and pharmaceuticals, "one third of the world's population still lacks access to essential drugs while in the poorest parts of Africa and Asia, over fifty percent of the population do not have regular access to the most vital essential drugs."[8] While the WHO notes that access to essential drugs doubled between 1977 and 1997—largely due to the adoption of essential drug lists and clinical treatment guidelines—it also emphasizes that securing access to essential medicines is dependent upon three critical factors: adequate financing, affordable prices, and reliable supply systems.[9]

The adoption and implementation of TRIPS in all countries after 2005, except the least developed countries (LDCs), has resulted in a new global intellectual property regime that places private interests before public need. While the Doha Declaration on the TRIPS Agreement and Public Health provides for some "flexibility" in the regime, the net effect is to require countries to either accept the primacy of private rights, in the form of intellectual property rights, or be prepared to declare national health emergencies, with all the resulting consequences for tourism and other economic and social policy concerns that rely on the projection of stable government and a healthy economy. Even if these broader public policy concerns are overlooked, the creation of a globalized private property regime in intellectual property has empowered the multinational pharmaceutical corporations and undermined the producers of "generic" versions of medicines, who earlier could rely on the particularities of domestic law—such as the distinction between product and process patents—to invest in research and production that would bring cheaper forms of the medicines onto the global market many years before the now-extended patent life of twenty years would end. The consequences of this shift, this chapter will argue, have dramatically changed the capacity of developing countries to provide essential medicines to their populations.

Finally, although a combination of aid, whether through the Global Fund or PEPFAR (the U.S. President's Emergency Plan for AIDS Relief), and generic and licensed production in India, Brazil, Thailand, and some other developing countries, such as South Africa, has led to a dramatic cut in the prices of first-line ARVs, it is the threat of antiretroviral treatment once again becoming prohibitively expensive that demands our attention. Now that the TRIPS regime has been implemented in all the producer countries, there is a danger that the only source of supply for the next generation of ARVs—particularly the second generation of drugs, which are already becoming an important fallback for patients who for one reason or another can no longer rely on the first-line treatments—will be solely in the hands of the originator companies. The lack of generic supply means that the second-line treatments are likely to remain prohibitively expensive for the full extent of the patent period—which under the TRIPS regime is extended to twenty years. Thus the present stalemate between the advocates of TRIPS-plus, those who would adopt a strict interpretation of TRIPS and the Doha Declaration, and those who seek ways to improve access to essential medicines, including the next generation of ARVs, remains a vital and urgent question that cannot be resolved by trade and patent laws but must become a central focus of both public health law and human rights. Simply asserting that sovereign countries may always declare an "emergency" as a means to provide access to essential medicines fails to recognize that the availability of affordable medicines involves much more than waiving the rules. Sustainable access to essential medicines involves long-term investment in productive generic capacity as well as quality and supply guarantees to ensure that these medicines are available to those who need them, when they are needed—forever in the case of ARVs for HIV-infected individuals—and at a cost that is affordable for both the affected individual and society at large.

TRANSFORMING INTELLECTUAL PROPERTY RIGHTS
THROUGH TRADE LAW

The international framework for patent rights evolved rapidly in the late twentieth century. Historically the protection of patent rights, while pursued internationally through the adoption of international agreements, was fundamentally a prerogative of national sovereignty. In fact, before the issue was put on the agenda at the Uruguay Round of trade talks in 1986, approximately forty states did not issue patents for pharmaceuticals, leading in some countries to a proliferation of copies of patented drugs. In other countries, such as India, the law recognized process patents in the pharmaceutical field but did not accept product patents. Since it is relatively easy for companies to find a different process to produce a given drug, the global pharmaceutical corporations have long sought product protection that would preclude the generics companies from simply reverse engineering a drug and finding an alternative means to produce it. However, at the international level the Paris and Berne Conventions impose only very general rules guaranteeing national treatment and most-favored-nation treatment to members but not the protection of all intellectual property rights. Thus the international regime of intellectual property protection prior to 1994 provided no guarantee of protection for intellectual property–intensive industries; instead, its protection depended upon the rights each jurisdiction offered its own citizens.

However, in the Uruguay Round of trade negotiations the intellectual property–intensive industries sought to achieve greater protection of their intellectual property rights and focused on creating a new international regime. While the 1970 Patent Cooperation Treaty had increased the World Intellectual Property Organization's (WIPO) institutional capacity to provide technical support services to national patent offices, the pharmaceutical industry continued to complain about commercial losses they attributed to the weakness of intellectual property rights protection, particularly in newly industrializing countries. For the pharmaceutical industry the goal was the establishment of minimum standards of patent protection allowing the increasingly multinational corporations that dominate the industry to operate in a single global market. The inclusion of the TRIPS Agreement as part of the founding of the World Trade Organization in 1994 was thus a major achievement for the advocates of a global standard of intellectual property rights, despite a history in which individual countries, including the United States, had used the granting of intellectual property rights as an incentive to promote their own historic processes of economic development and industrialization.

PLACING INTELLECTUAL PROPERTY RIGHTS ON THE GLOBAL AGENDA: THE ROLE OF PRIVATE INTERESTS

In 1982, intellectual property rights were raised in the context of international trade negotiations at the GATT (General Agreement on Tariffs and Trade) ministerial meeting. This was the first indication of the impact of a group of U.S. corporate leaders who in the late 1970s "devised a strategy to improve intellectual property protection internationally until American standards became the international norm, especially in developing countries."[10] According to Philip Ellsworth, a corporate leader and ex-chairman of the International Organizations and Issues Committee of the Pharmaceutical Manufacturers Association[11] in the United States, the industry pursued three avenues in its effort to achieve greater patent protection: first, a multilateral response aimed at the international organizations WIPO and GATT; second, a bilateral response asking the U.S. government to put pressure on trading partners to improve intellectual property protection; and finally, a unilateral approach through which the industry pushed for changes in U.S. law that both enabled and required the United States Trade Representative (USTR) to monitor the level of protection granted in countries around the world and to take action when the intellectual property rights of U.S. citizens were not being adequately protected.[12]

This strategy involved a number of distinct steps. First, Pfizer—one of the largest manufacturers of pharmaceuticals—attempted to achieve reform of the Paris Convention through WIPO. However, this effort was frustrated by a one-nation, one-vote decisionmaking procedure that empowered the opposition of developing countries. Subsequently, however, Pfizer began to work with other multinationals, such as IBM, to emphasize the need for U.S. trade negotiations to "go beyond purely trade policy matters and focus on obstacles to investment."[13] This was done through corporate participation in the Advisory Committee for Trade Policy and Negotiations, established by the 1974 Trade Act to institutionalize business input into U.S. trade policy and multilateral negotiations. It was this second step, bringing private interests into the realm of public decisionmaking, that would begin to reframe intellectual property protection as an issue of free trade with vast "implications for innovation, economic development, the future location of industry, and the global division of labour."[14]

As part of this effort, Pfizer worked with the Pharmaceutical Manufacturers of America to lobby Congress, the executive branch, and especially the USTR to promote increased protection for intellectual property rights abroad. The success of this domestic effort is evident in two distinct but complementary U.S. government initiatives. First, the USTR agreed to "expend the considerable diplomatic effort needed to put intellectual property on the GATT Uruguay Round agenda."[15] Thus when the Uruguay Round began in 1986, Pfizer's chief executive and the chairman of IBM established the Intellectual Property Committee to coordinate the policy of intellectual property–based corporations in the negotiations. Second, Congress amended the Trade Act three times — in 1979, 1984, and 1988 — increasing the power of the USTR to take retaliatory action against countries seen as engaging in "unfair" trade practices, even if the sanctions imposed would violate the international obligations of the United States.[16]

An important aspect of this new legal regime was the provision of formal procedures through which private parties could petition the USTR to vindicate the rights of U.S. citizens. Furthermore, the 1988 amendments included two statutory provisions, now popularly referred to as Special 301 and Super 301, that were particularly far-reaching. While Super 301 "required the US Trade Representative to identify and initiate Section 301 actions against foreign countries that used unfair trade practice to inhibit US trade," Special 301 requires the USTR, "on a yearly basis, to identify and initiate Section 301 actions against foreign counties that deny adequate and effective protection of intellectual property rights to US persons and products."[17] The power of Special 301 lies in the requirement that the USTR monitor and report annually on all foreign intellectual property laws and practices and in the "fast-track" system, which requires the USTR to decide on what retaliatory action to take within six months. This led to the creation of both a "priority watch list" and a "watch list" (in which the USTR names countries it believes are falling short in their protection of U.S. intellectual property rights and through which pressure is brought to bear in order to obtain higher levels of protection of intellectual property in those countries).

Early success was achieved in Korea, which, already in 1987, adopted both patent and pipeline (protection for existing inventions before a patent is formally granted) protection for pharmaceuticals.[18] However, beginning in 1991 the USTR took up a series of cases aimed at countries that boasted burgeoning domestic pharmaceutical manufacturing industries, most of which relied on reverse engineering to produce cheap forms of drugs initially developed in more industrialized countries. The first of these cases challenged Thailand's intellectual property regime. Despite U.S. acknowledgment that it was demanding higher standards than required under the existing international standards, Thailand revised its patent law in February 1992 to comply with these demands. In May 1991 the USTR also initiated an investigation of India's intellectual property laws, focusing particularly on the failure of Indian law to protect pharmaceutical products and its broad involuntary licensing provisions. After India refused to accede to U.S. demands, President Clinton partially suspended India's duty-free treatment under the Generalized System of Preferences, withdrawing $80 million in benefits on exports. At the same time, India was opposing aspects of the U.S.-sponsored TRIPS Agreement in the still ongoing Uruguay Round talks.

Canada provides another instructive example, targeted by the pharmaceutical industry for both its own internal policies and the example it provided for developing countries — in the words of Philip Ellsworth, who described Canadians as having a womb-to-tomb mentality: "Canada has a Third World mindset. It is a problem."[19] What Ellsworth was referring to was the Canadian policy of compulsory licensing for pharmaceuticals. Under Canadian law, pharmaceuticals were not covered by the regular patent provisions; rather, generics firms were able to apply to the government for a compulsory license to manufacture any pharmaceutical product, provided that they paid a royalty of 4% to the patent holder.[20] As Robert Sherwood, a U.S. expert on intellectual property law, told a November 1991 free trade conference organized by the University of Toronto's Centre for International Studies, the Pharmaceutical Manufacturer's Association was pushing the George H. W. Bush administration to achieve in the negotiations for the North American Free Trade Agreement (NAFTA) what it had failed to obtain in the earlier Free Trade Agreement with Canada. The issue, according to Sherwood, "was not so much Canada but the fact that developing countries were 'using Canada as an example to justify compulsory licensing as a means to achieve lower prescription-drug prices.'"[21] In fact the George H. W. Bush administration "made eliminating the Canadian law a condition for concluding" NAFTA.[22]

The United States negotiators in the NAFTA intellectual property negotiations had two basic aims: to prohibit discrimination among fields of technology, thus precluding a special regime for pharmaceuticals, and to narrow down the conditions under which it would be permissible to adopt compulsory licensing.[23] Responding to this pressure, the Canadian government conducted a Pharmaceutical Review in 1991, which concluded that competitive patent protection was needed in order to attract new investment and encourage research and development. Significantly, the Canadian pharmaceutical industry, while not in the first level of integrated firms — those engaged in R&D (research and development), manufacture, and distribution — does have innovative capacity and so could have considered this an opportunity for their own expansion. The Canadian government however decided not to merely accept U.S. demands but rather to support the Dunkel Text — the GATT package proposed in December 1991 by Arthur Dunkel, GATT's director-general. By demanding that NAFTA reflect the GATT, Canada could endorse full patent protection for pharmaceuticals but also avoid issues, such as parallel imports, that are left aside by TRIPS. NAFTA in fact ignores the parallel imports issue and leaves it to the parties to ban them through their own domestic legislation if they so wish.[24]

As a result, Canadian legislation adopted in February 1993 abolished the special regime for compulsory licensing for pharmaceuticals, providing instead for full patent protection for applications filed in Canada on or after October 1, 1989.[25] The legislation however also gave the Patented Medicine Prices Review Board (PMPRB) the power to order fines and to lower prices of patented medicines. As the WTO noted in its Trade Policy Review of Canada in 1998, "the guidelines issued by the PMPRB limit prices of most new patented drugs to the range of prices for existing drugs used in the treatment of the same disease; to the median of the prices charged for the drug in other industrialized countries and to increases in the consumer price index (for patented drugs already on the market)."[26] Although the Canadian scheme remains contested — involving at least two decisions by the WTO panel in 2000 — Canada has thus far managed to resist accepting the TRIPS-plus standards of total patent protection demanded by the United States government.

Despite these gains through the use of U.S. domestic law and bilateral negotiations, the pharmaceutical industry's strategy to enforce intellectual property rights through the international trade regime continued to face strong opposition, especially from developing and newly industrialized countries.[27] However, a new form of multilateral negotiating, linking bargaining over different issues, combined with an international agreement that membership in the new World Trade Organization would require acceptance of a single package, provided the basis for inclusion of intellectual property rights in the final 1994 agreement that came out of the Uruguay Round. The adoption of the TRIPS Agreement as part of that new world trade regime fundamentally changed the global legal environment for the production and supply of medicines.

PUBLIC HEALTH AND FREE TRADE

Although intellectual property rights (IPRs) were raised for the first time in the context of international trade negotiations at the 1982 ministerial meeting of the GATT, it would take until 1986 before IPRs would be a formal part of the Uruguay Round agenda. While the linking of intellectual property and trade issues may be traced to structural and legal changes affecting patents and intellectual property more generally within the United States—including the roles of technology, deregulation, and the creation of the patent court in 1982[28]—it was the Canadian proposal in October 1990 "that the new Multilateral Trade Organization (MTO) should be acceded to as a single undertaking"[29] that set the stage for the successful integration of intellectual property rights into the international trade regime. Although some developing nations and newly industrialized countries objected to the inclusion of intellectual property as part of the subject matter of negotiations,[30] it was this change in the format of negotiations that sealed the outcome of these already contentious debates. Previously, under the GATT, each tariff reduction or other measure aimed at reducing barriers to international trade would be individually negotiated, and countries could agree to be party to different elements of the GATT without being bound by all its provisions. Negotiating a single package on the basis of a negotiated consensus had the effect of transforming the entire international trade regime.

Since the Second World War, it may have been assumed that public health issues, particularly those with transnational effects, would be coordinated by the WHO as the relevant body within the United Nations system. The WHO constitution empowered the organization's governing body, the World Health Assembly, to adopt conventions as well as other international legal instruments, including binding regulations.[31] In practice, however, the WHO has, until very recently, relied more on the adoption of standards, principles, and models supplemented by the body's annual reports and occasional declarations, such as the Alma-Ata Declaration, which called upon countries and international organizations to adopt a system of primary health care.[32] When it came to the regulation of pharmaceuticals, the essential medicines program exemplified the WHO's choice of standards rather than rules. Any binding legal rules controlling the availability of medicines remained rooted in two independent legal processes within national jurisdictions, one regulatory and the other based on the laws of the market, including the relevant intellectual property rules of each country.

Despite a long history of the international regulation of drugs,[33] the availability of any particular medicine still depends on its registration by the health authorities or other agencies empowered to decide which products meet the required standards of safety and effectiveness. Even after registration, access to these drugs depends on their affordability in the market and, for the vast majority of patients in the developing world, on whether the state is able to make the drugs available through the public health system. In this latter case, states have mostly relied on the availability of generic substitutes or used their relative market power to bargain for sustainable public-sector prices. Despite the state's formal status as sovereign power, many developing countries, particularly in Africa, in the era of structural adjustment and neoliberal fiscal constraints, have lost the capacity to keep their public hospital dispensaries well stocked. The implementation of national essential drugs programs that rely to a large extent on the model lists produced by the WHO had provided one mechanism for governments to manage the supply, use, and cost of pharmaceuticals.

CHANGED CIRCUMSTANCES

The introduction of lifesaving antiretroviral medicines in 1996, coming only two years after the adoption of the new WTO trade regime at Marrakesh in April 1994, simultaneously gave new hope to those engulfed in the pandemic and raised questions about the cost and availability of these new drug regimes. Although many countries had adopted the WHO's essential drugs program model as a means to provide greater access to medicines for all ailments, it was the fact that these new drugs were dramatically reducing mortality rates among HIV/AIDS patients in developed countries and would have to be taken for the rest of a patient's life that made them the key focus of activists around the world. The struggle to guarantee access to these medicines soon unfolded at multiple levels: locally, in the form of the Treatment Action Campaign in South Africa and ACT UP in the United States; internationally, in the campaigns of international non-governmental organizations, such as Doctors Without Borders/Médecins Sans Frontières and Oxfam; and on the global stage, as developing country governments pointed to the public health exceptions in the TRIPS Agreement and demanded recognition of these flexibilities through the Doha Declaration in 2001.

The building of a new transnational solidarity in the face of HIV/AIDS[34] transformed the terrain upon which the struggle over access to medicines continues, but this effort has also been corralled by the emergence of philanthropic initiatives and strategic licensing by the pharmaceutical corporations. At the same time, some developing countries, such as Brazil and Thailand, continue to resist attempts to undermine their domestic pharmaceutical industries and have taken advantage of the debate over access to pursue their own industrial strategies around pharmaceutical production. Even South Africa, which has not had a major pharmaceutical industry, has begun to explore ways in which the changing regime of exceptions for least developed countries and regional procurement might bolster the country's economic ambitions.

During the 1990s, however, initiatives affecting health care, particularly within individual nations, seemed to have shifted away from reliance on WHO standards and toward incorporation of decisions made by a range of other international bodies, including the World Bank and the WTO.[35] Fueled by the debate over access to medicines in the context of the HIV/AIDS pandemic, the question of the relationship between health and trade policies began to complicate the WTO's trade agenda in the late 1990s. Launching the Doha Round of Multilateral Trade Negotiations in November 2001 was however only made possible after members agreed to adopt the Doha Declaration on the TRIPS Agreement and Public Health. Despite concerted opposition from multinational pharmaceutical corporations and a group of developed countries led by the United States, Switzerland, and Japan, the 140 trade ministers gathered in Doha, Qatar, agreed that the TRIPS Agreement "does not and should not prevent Members from taking measures to protect public health...[and] that the Agreement can and should be interpreted and implemented in a manner supportive of WTO Members' rights to protect public health and, in particular, to promote access to medicines for all."

At first blush, this seemed to be a major negotiating success for the developing world. Not only was this interpretation extended to all aspects of public health, not just pharmaceuticals, but it also emphasized the need to interpret the WTO agreements in more holistic ways. In essence, it accepted that an interpretation reducing barriers to free trade is not automatically the sole or correct understanding of the relevant agreements. The United States and Canada opposed any broad public health exception, but their own threats to override Bayer's Cipro patent—in response to the mailed anthrax attacks[36]—weakened their official claims that the strong protection of patents was the most effective means of securing access to required medicines. The Doha Declaration specifically recognizes the rights of a member state to grant compulsory licenses, to determine what constitutes a national emergency or other circumstance of extreme urgency, and to establish its own regime for the exhaustion of intellectual property rights. It also encourages developed countries to promote technology transfer to the least developed countries, and it extends the initial transition period, with respect to pharmaceutical products, until January 1, 2016. The understanding of the TRIPS Agreement reached in Doha constituted a major shift in the rhetoric about the protection of intellectual property rights; yet, given the realities of pharmaceutical production and distribution, little progress has been made toward actually ensuring access to urgently needed HIV/AIDS-related medications.

Despite acknowledging that many countries have "insufficient or no manufacturing capacities in the pharmaceutical sector" and thus cannot make effective use of compulsory licensing, the declaration failed to accept the developing countries' claim that they have the right to grant compulsory licenses to producers in countries with greater manufacturing capacity in order to gain access to medicines. Instead, the declaration instructed the TRIPS Council to find a solution and to report to the WTO General Council by the end of 2002. Without the capacity to produce under compulsory licenses or to import generic equivalents of necessary medications, the problem of access for the millions infected with or suffering from life-threatening diseases in developing countries remained unresolved. It took the TRIPS Council twenty-one more months to finally reach agreement in late August 2003 on the problem of access to medicines for countries that lack manufacturing capacity, which includes most countries in sub-Saharan Africa. (Even South Africa, which has a limited pharmaceutical industry and the capacity to manufacture ARVs, imports 100% of the active pharmaceutical ingredients.) Heralded at first as the solution to the problem of lack of capacity, that pre-Cancun agreement has since been criticized as being unworkable for placing so many prerequisites on its implementation. Before it can benefit from this agreement, which has now been formalized by the WTO, a country must prove that it lacks production capacity and access to affordable medicines and that it has an existing health emergency. While the Canadian government has taken steps to change Canadian law to make the export of medicines produced under these compulsory licenses possible, the international brand-name pharmaceutical industry has begun to raise questions about whether NAFTA precludes Canada from supplying these medicines. Even the Canadian government itself seems to be limiting its proposals to drugs designed to address HIV/ AIDS, malaria, and tuberculosis, a restriction rejected by the developing countries and the pre-Cancun agreement.[37] Over six years later this mechanism has only been used once, by Rwanda, which has placed a limited order with a Canadian company.

Within legal discourse the claims of the international patent-based pharmaceutical corporations were framed as rights to property, while the claims of developing country governments and non-governmental organizations seeking access to affordable medicines were characterized as legal exceptions to free trade or as soft law reflecting norms and standards contained in general preambular clauses, resolutions, and statements. These formal legal distinctions, based upon the interpretation of international agreements created in a context of asymmetrical power, are now relied upon to delay and avoid recognizing the urgent needs of those whose very lives and futures are at stake. At the same time the price of first-generation ARVs has dropped due to the introduction of generic versions of these medicines.[38] While the dramatic reduction in prices has enabled developing countries to adopt a more comprehensive response to the HIV/AIDS pandemic, the transformation of the international patent regime means that in the case of second-generation ARVs, which are becoming increasingly important in the treatment of HIV/AIDS, such generics competition is unlikely to emerge.

PUBLIC GOODS, PHARMACEUTICALS, AND ACCESS TO ESSENTIAL MEDICINES

While it is clearly true that drug prices are not the only issue limiting access to essential medicines in developing countries, the cost of medicines remains a central concern because unlike the broader structural problems of upgrading the health-care system or monitoring patients, there are just no substitutes for or alternatives to the provision of these particular drugs. In the case of HIV/AIDS, an estimated two-thirds of the 33.2 million people living with HIV at the end of 2007 lived in sub-Saharan Africa, and even with a tenfold increase in those receiving access to ARVs over a five-year period, only 42% of those in need of ARVs are receiving treatment.[39] To this extent the cost of the medicines is in fact the "inelastic" part of the essential medicines equation. Yet even as innovative programs have been designed to facilitate access to health care, monitoring, and so forth,[40] the debate over drug costs has focused on collective purchasing strategies, philanthropic initiatives, and international assistance or aid rather than on the creation of a competitive market, which would be the most effective way to reduce prices and increase supply. Nevertheless first-generation ARV prices have fallen dramatically from around $10,000 per patient per year in the late 1990s to around $99 today, in some cases.[41] The actual cost of providing "free" drugs, even through many of the philanthropic schemes, remains slightly above the actual cost of large-scale generic production and distribution because of the insistence by developed country governments that these medicines be either purchased from the brand-name firms or their licensed producers, in the case of PEPFAR, or specifically marked and packaged so as to avoid their illegal re-importation and distribution in developed country markets. Even as prices have dropped and aid increased, the question has arisen as to whether these developments will be able to assure a stable supply of ARV medicines. Given the fact that there is no known cure, a stable and affordable supply of these medications is essential to the productive lives of millions of HIV-positive individuals around the world, and particularly in developing countries.

In order to evaluate the stability of any policy or program to provide access to affordable essential medicines, it is important to briefly review the political pressures and alternative sources of supply that have brought down the cost of these medicines over the last few years. First, it was the offer by Indian drug producer Cipla in March 2001 to provide the first-generation ARV drugs for $350 per patient per year to developing countries, a fraction of the going price in the developed country markets, that brought about the initial fall in prices.[42] Although Brazil had already managed to reduce the price from $10,000 per patient to around $2800 per patient within its own public health system, this was based on the government-controlled industry's capacity to reverse engineer and manufacture the relevant drugs. Second, it was the accusations of activists and the bad publicity that multinational drug companies received after they sued the South African government and named President Mandela as the first defendant that led to offers by these companies to supply drugs to some developing countries at vastly reduced costs, and in some cases at no cost, for certain periods of time and for specified classes of poor patients. Third, the establishment of the Global Fund and later President Bush's PEPFAR initiative provided a source of funding for anti-AIDS programs, including the provision of essential medicines in the public sector. Fourth, the entry of the Gates and Clinton Foundations both as funders and as sources of political coordination of efforts aimed at the procurement of cheaper drugs bolstered the longstanding efforts of non-governmental organizations, such as Doctors Without Borders, James Love's Consumer Project on Technology, the Canadian HIV/AIDS Legal Network, and the AIDS Law Project in South Africa, as well as various AIDS-specific activist organizations, such as ACT UP in the United States and the South Africa–based Treatment Action Campaign. Finally, the establishment in 2006 of UNITAID, the international drug purchase facility initiated by the governments of Brazil, France, and Norway, promised a long-term source of funding through a type of Tobin tax on international airline ticket sales and an international organization committed to pooling demand and using the resulting bargaining power to obtain medicines at reduced cost in the international market.[43]

While these different initiatives have very different protagonists and modes of operation, the underlying premise of all these strategies is the continued existence of an adequate supply of the required medicines at affordable prices. Already there have been a number of incidents in which the supply of ARVs has been interrupted, with obvious dire consequences for individual patients in addition to the possibility of drug resistance developing in those patients unable to maintain their treatment programs. In the case of the ARV ritonavir, for example, there were five occasions in 2004 when drug companies in South Africa were unable to supply the drug in either pediatric doses or adult capsules, forcing patients to switch their medications and leading the South African government to briefly halt the rollout of their public-sector program for children.[44] These incidents and concern over the cost of second-line drugs as well as the WHO's new treatment guidelines that suggest the use of more expensive drugs[45] all raise questions about the stability and sustainability of the supply chain of affordable drugs. In order to understand the magnitude of this problem, it is important to note two facts: first, that under normal conditions the cost of a patented drug drops by only 20% when the first generic enters the market at the end of the patent term; and second, that it is only when there are three or more generics companies competing to supply a particular drug that the cost falls to anywhere between 70% and 90% below the original price of the patented drug.[46]

Until 2005 this was not a dramatic problem because Indian drug producers were able to produce generic versions of these medicines so long as they were able to come up with a process of production that had not been previously patented. As a result Indian pharmaceutical companies have in recent years been producing approximately "one-fifth of the world's generic drugs."[47] The implementation of the TRIPS Agreement in India since January 2005, which required the reintroduction of product patents into Indian law, now precludes the possibility that these companies will be able to produce generic versions of the next generation of ARVs, and henceforth the only way these companies will be able to enter the market to provide generic forms of any new drugs will be as licensed-producers, whether under voluntary or compulsory licenses.[48] This will both limit the number of companies that may enter the market and isolate the originator companies from competition for as long as they can maintain their monopoly power through patent claims and/or strategic licensing. In South Africa the brand-name companies have increasingly licensed local manufacturers to produce their products for the local and regional markets. Most prominent of these companies is Aspen Pharmacare, whose main aim is to acquire patent-expired medicines from multinational drug firms and which now controls 35% of South Africa's generic drug market.[49] While the turn to local licensing may have been made in the face of growing international pressure and after settling the case against them before South Africa's Competition Commission, a number of the brand-name companies have now licensed Aspen to locally manufacture their products. Aspen has in turn succeeded in having its newly constructed oral solid dosage plant in the Eastern Cape region of South Africa approved by both the "local regulator, the Medicines Control Council, [and]...the American Food & Drug Administration and the UK's Medical Health & Regulatory Authority."[50] This placed the company in a position not only to win the South African state tender in 2004, producing R3.4bn in ARV drugs over three years, but also to potentially win large international aid contracts with PEPFAR and the Global Fund.[51]

While the Brazilian and Thai governments have stood up to pressures from the United States and multinational drug companies by either issuing compulsory licenses for the local production of needed medicines or negotiating local licenses and affordable prices under the threat of compulsory licensing, these options require either a state-owned pharmaceutical producer, as in the case of Brazil, or the political courage to take on the industry, as Thailand has recently done. In both these cases the target has been domestic supply coupled with local production capacity, which is well protected by the Doha Declaration. The problem for most developing countries is that they either lack domestic production capacity altogether or their internal markets are too small to sustain the level of production that is needed to gain the cost-cutting benefits of large-scale production. While Paragraph 6 negotiations and subsequent amendment to the TRIPS Agreement were supposed to address this difficulty, the failure of countries to make wide use of these provisions indicates that there is substance to the claim of critics that the "safeguards" insisted upon by the developed countries and multinational drug companies have in fact proved too burdensome and undermined the effectiveness of this solution. Despite the falling prices, company giveaways, and philanthropic efforts, Oxfam has recently noted that "the inability of the Paragraph 6 solution to deliver medicines is a serious threat to the legitimacy of the WTO."[52] Furthermore, despite the designation of health as a priority in the United Nations Millennium Development Goals adopted by world leaders in 2000 and the Doha Declaration adopted in November 2001, more than twenty million more people have been infected with HIV in the twenty-first century, and the cost of medicine still "represents that greatest share of health-care expenditures for people in poor countries."[53]

HUMAN RIGHTS AND ESSENTIAL MEDICINES

Until recently, public health and the obligation of government to provide for collective health needs have been understood only in terms of measures that are necessary to prevent large-scale epidemics. This preventive approach is evident in the development of the idea of primary health care, which "is a blend of essential health services, personal responsibility for one's own health and health-promoting action taken by the community."[54] The most effective means for achieving public health goals have been the provision of clean water, good sanitation, and more recently, widespread vaccination. While these remain the most cost-effective and broadly applicable ways to protect public health, the revolution in pharmaceuticals during the twentieth century has blurred the line between treatment and prevention. In the context of the HIV/AIDS pandemic, where prevention on its own has proven extremely difficult, the most effective approach seems to lie in the combination of preventive education, treatment, and the lowering of individuals' viral loads. Effective prevention must include treatment, and today, particularly in developing countries, this requires access to affordable medicines, which are now understood to be integral to the achievement of public health goals.

At the beginning of the twentieth century, "aspirin was the only widely available modern medicine,"[55] but by the 1970s modern pharmaceuticals existed for nearly every major illness known to medical science.

The problem was clearly one of access. It was in response to this situation that the idea of identifying a list of essential medicines arose and led to the launch of the WHO's essential medicines program in 1977. The program produced model lists of essential drugs that national governments use to make their own local lists; these lists make the task of providing prescribed medications more manageable by limiting the thousands of available medicines to approximately two hundred essential ones. By the turn of the century, over 160 countries had adopted essential drug lists and clinical treatment guidelines based on the WHO's model lists and selection criteria, which effectively doubled access to essential medicines. The criteria laid out for compiling these lists reflect a synergetic amalgam of public health and human rights concerns, with an emphasis on equal access and medical effectiveness. Drugs chosen for an essential medicines list must "satisfy the health needs of the majority of the population; be available at all times in adequate amounts and appropriate dosage forms; and be available at a price that individuals and the community can afford."[56] When it comes to choosing between different available drugs, there are five key criteria: relative efficacy, safety, quality, price, and availability. Reliance on these criteria has led to an emphasis on off-patent, or generic, drugs, which still comprise more than 90% of the medicines included on the model list.[57]

While the price of pharmaceuticals varies significantly between different markets, the cost of most patented medicines remains beyond the reach of the bulk of the population in developing countries. This reality is starkly evident in the case of HIV/AIDS, where the emergence of drug regimes to manage the disease in the mid 1980s created a bifurcated epidemic. Opening the Thirteenth International AIDS Conference in Durban, South African high court judge Edwin Cameron claimed to embody "the injustice of AIDS in Africa because, on a continent in which 290 million Africans survive on less than one U.S. dollar a day, I can afford medication costs of about $400 per month."[58] Accusing manufacturers of imposing prices that made drugs "unaffordably expensive," Cameron argued that the international patent and trade regime prevents the production and marketing of affordable drugs, despite earlier experience in India, Thailand, and Brazil that demonstrates the feasibility of producing key drugs at costs within reach of the developing world.[59]

Still today, despite a dramatic drop in the price of antiretrovirals, victims of the HIV/AIDS pandemic may be divided into those for whom contraction of HIV remains a death sentence and those for whom the disease is a chronic illness they are able to manage. The disparity in access to antiretrovirals that creates this divide is heightened by the lack of generic alternatives, which has fueled the demand for access to medicines in general and generic drugs in particular. Using affordability as one of the relevant criteria, the essential drug program promoted the use of generic drugs, a strategy that allowed the program to both limit costs and reduce conflict with the global patent-based pharmaceutical industry, which opposes generic substitution (particularly for products originating from countries that did not recognize the companies' product patents). The inclusion of twelve antiretrovirals on the WHO's model essential medicines list in 2002[60] brought this tension to the fore and made it clear that the program's primary reliance on generics for the effective delivery of affordable drugs was no longer tenable as all the available ARVs were at that time under patent protection.

Access to essential drugs, from this perspective, becomes a critical part of the fundamental human right to health.[61] While the WHO accepts that "patent protection stimulates development of needed new drugs," it argues that "countries must ensure a balance between the interests of the patent holders and the needs of society." Advocating that "generic competition should begin promptly upon patent expiration" and that "preferential pricing is necessary for lower-income countries and should be actively pursued,[62] the WHO also argues that because the research and development priorities of the pharmaceutical industry do not necessarily respond to the needs of the bulk of the world's population, there should be public involvement to "ensure development of new drugs for certain priority health problems."[63] Thus, although the WHO does not reject the idea of pharmaceutical patents, its position seems to question the unbridled power of private decisionmaking in the research effort and to claim some level of exception to the rights of patent holders for essential drugs. This prioritization of health over specific property rights becomes the key to a human rights approach.

While legal frameworks are often focused on the allocation and protection of rights, it is important to recall that the human rights approach is premised on the dual notions of dignity and rights. Article 1 of the Universal Declaration of Human Rights adopted by the UN General

Assembly states that "all human beings are born free and equal in dignity and rights. They are endowed with reason and conscience and should act towards one another in a spirit of brotherhood." It is from this premise that a human rights approach must recognize the conflicting rights to health and property that are inherent in our present framing of the debate over access to essential medicines. Equal recognition of the status of human dignity, as well as the Universal Declaration's linking of dignity and rights to the duty of solidarity, provides a balanced approach—from a human rights perspective—to the question of where the emphasis should fall in any conflict between the property rights of some and the health of others.

The failure to recognize the demands of human solidarity may be seen in the bureaucratic actions of Dutch customs authorities in the port of Rotterdam who seized a shipment of a generic drug to treat high blood pressure that was en route to Brazil in early December 2008. Responding to claims that the drugs being shipped between India and Brazil violated patent rights registered in the Netherlands, the Dutch authorities maintained that all goods in transit through Europe are fully subject to the European regulatory regime. In response India and Brazil expressed outrage in both the WHO and the WTO, arguing that by acting at the behest of the company owning patent rights to the drug in the Netherlands, the Dutch authorities had refused to recognize the flexibilities inherent in the TRIPS Agreement or the various resolutions by the WHO stating that the health needs of member states should be upheld ahead of intellectual property claimants. The Dutch authorities impounded the drugs for over a month and then sent them back to India, where they had been manufactured, despite the fact that the property rights at issue did not exist in either India or Brazil.[64] Here the dignity of those patients in need of access to these medicines was wantonly ignored in a logic that sought to resolve the rights of the different claimants without acknowledging the countervailing issues of dignity inherent in the effort to restore health to individuals, families, and communities.

CONCLUSION

In the realm of international trade law it seems that the question of access to essential medicines is being constantly displaced by an assertion of prior legal commitments — the idea of *pacta sunt servanda* — in which concerns over the rights of patent holders and an interpretation of the TRIPS Agreement as a contractual arrangement place notions of unrestricted free trade before the health needs of millions of people around the world. While all participants in the debate deny any intention to restrict access, or even such an effect,[65] it seems hard to deny that the failure to resolve this issue, since it was first raised by the international pharmaceutical industry in its 1997 case against the South African law that attempted to implement an essential drugs program, has in fact frustrated attempts to broaden access. Even if it is accepted that the TRIPS Agreement initially failed to accommodate the complexities of a global health emergency such as HIV/AIDS, it is hardly unreasonable to suggest that the principle of changed circumstances — or rebus sic stantibus — brought about by new understandings of the magnitude of the pandemic as well as the emergence of effective medicines to address it, should have been applied to interpretations of TRIPS in order to facilitate all attempts to address this exploding crisis. At the very least, such an approach would justify the assertion of an Article 30 general exception under the TRIPS Agreement. Instead, there has been a constant emphasis upon the rather unique protection of private rights contained in TRIPS and a denial of the legal effect of the so-called soft-law exceptions and principles of interpretation that are also part of international trade law, including TRIPS.

In this Kafkaesque world of legal wrangling over exceptions, counter-exceptions, and sacrosanct rules, it is important to assert a human rights perspective that might overcome the paradox of lifesaving medicines that might be easily produced at minimal cost and the failure of social solidarity that tolerates the rationing of these scientific benefits on the grounds that only extraordinary profits for the global pharmaceutical industry will guarantee the future discovery of miracle drugs. While there is heated debate over the real cost of pharmaceuticals and the system of innovation,[66] with some arguing that public funding of the basic science is still the fundamental source of scientific breakthroughs and that in the context of medicines some type of prize might be a better way to stimulate innovation than granting a patent monopoly, it seems to me that in the face of a global pandemic, such as HIV/AIDS, it is important to recognize first that medicines are fundamentally public goods.[67]

Furthermore, if we acknowledge that the price of the drugs is directly related to the number of firms or generics in the market, then it is important to promote legal certainty so as to encourage as many pharmaceutical producers as possible to invest in the production of these drugs. Instead of a very limited provision aimed at allowing countries who can show they do not have production capacity to issue limited compulsory licenses and to seek the issuing of a corresponding license in a country with production capacity, as is the case under the Paragraph 6 mechanism, it is important that either a general exception for public health needs be asserted under Article 30 of the TRIPS Agreement or developing countries be mobilized to reject the strictures of TRIPS and guarantee that they will protect the right of generics companies to continue to produce the needed drugs, including if necessary the reverse engineering and production of the new second generation of HIV/AIDS drugs that will otherwise be subject to global patent monopoly for the next twenty years. While 97% of adults and children presently on ARV therapy are receiving first-line medications, problems of drug resistance and individual clinical changes mean that an increasing number of people living with HIV will have to have access to the second generation of drugs in the years ahead.

Finally, while recognizing the need to regulate the quality of medicines, the global diffusion of the institution of product patents in particular might be seriously questioned. On the one hand, the TRIPS Agreement that facilitated this diffusion was agreed upon in 1994, nearly two years before an effective pharmaceutical response to HIV/AIDS had been discovered and brought to bear against the pandemic, while on the other hand, the pre-2005 existence of process patents in the Indian context had the effect of both stimulating generic production and limiting the impact of a patent monopoly over lifesaving medicines. This suggests that, at the minimum, a reversion to a more limited intellectual property regime in the context of public health might achieve a better balance between the various national and private interests that have been the focus of TRIPS and the demands of a more human solidarity that might bring hope to millions of people whose lives are indelibly marked by the burden of diseases that in other circumstances might be managed so that they can remain valued members of their communities and productive citizens of their countries.

NOTES

1   Greg Behrman, *The Invisible People: How the U.S. Has Slept Through the Global AIDS Pandemic, the Greatest Humanitarian Catastrophe of Our Time* (New York: Free Press, 2004), xiii.

2   Graham Dutfield, *Intellectual Property Rights and the Life Science Industries: A Twentieth Century History* (Aldershot, UK: Ashgate, 2003), 92–97.

3   Joint United Nations Programme on HIV/AIDS and World Health Organization, *AIDS Epidemic Update: December 2007* (Geneva: UNAIDS / WHO, 2007).

4   Heinz Klug, "Campaigning for Life: Building a New Transnational Solidarity in the Face of HIV/AIDS and TRIPS," in *Law and Globalization from Below: Towards a Cosmopolitan Legality*, ed. Boaventura de Sousa Santos and César A. Rodríguez-Garavito (Cambridge: Cambridge University Press, 2005).

5   Michael Ryan, *Knowledge Diplomacy: Global Competition and the Politics of Intellectual Property* (Washington, DC: Brookings Institution, 1998), 5.

6   Gro Harlem Brundtland, "International Trade Agreements and Public Health: WHO's Role" (WHO director-general video address at the Conference on Increasing Access to Essential Drugs in a Globalised Economy, Amsterdam, November 25–26, 1999), http://www.who.int/director-general/speeches/1999/english/19991125_amsterdam.html.

7   Jonathan M. Mann et al., eds., *Health and Human Rights: A Reader* (New York: Routledge, 1999).

8   Michael Scholtz, "International Trade Agreements and Public Health: WHO's Role" (paper presented at the Conference on Increasing Access to Essential Drugs in a Globalised Economy, Amsterdam, November 25–26, 1999), http://www.haiweb.org/campaign/novseminar/scholtz.html.

9   Ibid.

10   Ryan, *Knowledge Diplomacy*, 68.

11   In 1994, the Pharmaceutical Manufacturers Association (PMA) became the Pharmaceutical Research and Manufacturers of America (PhRMA).

12   Lee A. Tavis and Oliver F. Williams, eds., *The Pharmaceutical Corporate Presence in Developing Countries* (Notre Dame, IN: University of Notre Dame Press, 1993), 198.

13   Ibid.

14   Susan K. Sell, "Structures, Agents and Institutions: Private Corporate Power and the Globalisation of Intellectual Property Rights," in *Non-State Actors and Authority in the Global System*, ed. Richard A. Higgott, Geoffrey R. D. Underhill, and Andreas Bieler (London: Routledge, 1999), 92.

15   Ryan, *Knowledge Diplomacy*, 69.

16 John H. Jackson, William J. Davey, and Alan O. Sykes, Jr., *Legal Problems of International Economic Relations: Cases, Materials and Text*, 3rd ed. (Eagan, MN: West, 1995), 818.

17 Ted L. McDorman, "U.S.–Thailand Trade Disputes: Applying Section 301 to Cigarettes and Intellectual Property," *Michigan Journal of International Law* 14 (1992): 96.

18 Tavis and Williams, *Pharmaceutical Corporate Presence*, 199.

19 Ibid., 200.

20 Maryse Robert, *Negotiating NAFTA: Explaining the Outcome in Culture, Textiles, Autos, and Pharmaceuticals* (Toronto: University of Toronto Press, 2000), 207.

21 Ibid., 238.

22 See Milt Freudenheim, "Canadians See Rise in Drug Costs," *New York Times*, November 16, 1992; and Robert, *Negotiating NAFTA*, 239.

23 Robert, *Negotiating NAFTA*, 208.

24 Ibid., 242.

25 Ibid., 224.

26 Ibid., 225.

27 See Ruth L. Gana, "The Myth of Development, The Progress of Rights: Human Rights to Intellectual Property and Development," *Law and Policy* 18 (1996): 315–54. See also Martin Adelman and Sonia Baldia, "Prospects and Limits of the Patent Provision in the TRIPS Agreement: The Case of India," Vanderbilt Journal of Transnational Law 29 (1996): 507–33.

28 See Susan K. Sell, *Private Power, Public Law: The Globalization of Intellectual Property Rights* (Cambridge: Cambridge University Press, 2003), 67–72.

29 Jayashree Watal, *Intellectual Property Rights in the WTO and Developing Countries* (The Hague: Kluwer Law International, 2001), 34.

30 See Gana, "Myth of Development"; and Adelman and Baldia, "Prospects and Limits."

31 David P. Fidler, *International Law and Public Health: Materials on and Analysis of Global Health Jurisprudence* (Ardsley, NY: Transnational Publishers, 2000), 118.

32 International Conference on Primary Health Care, "Declaration of Alma-Ata," *Primary Health Care: Report of the International Conference* (Geneva: WHO / UNICEF, 1978).

33 John Braithwaite and Peter Drahos, *Global Business Regulation* (Cambridge: Cambridge University Press, 2000), 360–98.

34 Klug, "Campaigning for Life."

35 Gill Walt, *Health Policy: An Introduction to Process and Power* (Johannesburg: Witwatersrand University Press, 1994); and Gill Walt, "Globalisation of International Health," *Lancet* 351, no. 9100 (1998): 434.

36 See Paul Blustein, "Drug Patents Dispute Poses Trade Threat; Generics Fight Could Derail WTO Accord," *Washington Post*, October 26, 2001. See also Kavaljit Singh, "Anthrax, Drug Transnationals and TRIPS: Profits Before Public Health," *Z Magazine*, December 2001: 39–42.

37 Canadian HIV/AIDS Legal Network, "Canada Proceeds with Bill C-9 on Cheaper Medicines Exports: NGOs Say Initiative Is Important, and Urge Other Countries To Avoid the Flaws in the Canadian Model," news release, April 28, 2004.

38 Médecins Sans Frontières, Campaign for Access to Essential Medicines, *Untangling the Web of Price Reductions: A Pricing Guide for the Purchase of ARVs for Developing Countries*, 10th ed. (Geneva: MSF, July 2007).

39 World Health Organization, *Towards Universal Access: Scaling Up Priority HIV/AIDS Interventions In the Health Sector, Progress Report 2009* (Geneva: WHO, 2009), 5.

40 World Health Organization, *Scaling Up Antiretroviral Therapy in Resource-Limited Settings: Treatment Guidelines for a Public Health Approach*, 2003 Revision (Geneva: WHO, 2004), http://www.who.int/hiv/pub/prev_care/en/arvrevision2003en.pdf.

41 Médecins Sans Frontières, *Untangling the Web*.

42 Ibid.

43 While Chile and the United Kingdom also participated in the launch of UNITAID, it was Brazil, France, and Norway that adopted the Tobin Tax approach.

44 See Jonathan Berger (AIDS Law Project) letter to Angelo Kondes (CEO of Abbot Labs, South Africa) regarding shortages of ritonavir, February 14, 2005, AIDS Law Project archives, Johannesburg, South Africa.

45 Médecins Sans Frontières, *Untangling the Web*.

46 Jacqui Pile, "Aspen Pharmacare: Clinical Coup," *Financial Mail* 182, no. 3 (July 15, 2005): 18.

47 Bruce Stokes, "Pachyderm Pharma," *National Journal*, April 16, 2005: 1146–50.

48 Kenneth C. Shadlen, "The Political Economy of AIDS Treatment: Intellectual Property and the Transformation of Generic Supply," *International Studies Quarterly* 51, no. 3 (2007): 559–81.

49 Pile, "Aspen Pharmacare."

50 Ibid., 19.

51 Ibid., 20.

52 Oxfam International, "Patents Versus Patients: Five Years After the Doha Declaration," Oxfam Briefing Paper 95 (Oxford: Oxfam International, 2006), 19.

53 Ibid., 7–8.

54 World Health Organization (WHO), *Concepts of Health Development* (Geneva: WHO, 1998), www.who.int/archives/who50/en/concepts.htm (accessed October 3, 2003).

55 Scholtz, "International Trade Agreements."

56 WHO, *Concepts of Health Development.*

57 World Health Organization, *The Use of Essential Drugs: Ninth Report of the WHO Expert Committee/Eleventh Model List of Essential Drugs*, Technical Report Series No. 895 (Geneva: WHO, 2000).

58 Edwin Cameron, "The Deafening Silence of AIDS" (First Jonathan Mann Memorial Lecture, 13th International AIDS Conference, Durban, South Africa, July 10, 2000), *Treatment Action Campaign News*, July 17, 2000, http://www.tac.org.za/newsletter/2000/ns000717.txt.

59 Ibid.

60 World Health Organization, "Updating and Disseminating the WHO Model List of Essential Drugs: The Way Forward" (draft, June 22, 2001). See also World Health Organization, *Medicines Strategy: 2000–2003*, WHO Policy Perspectives on Medicines No. 1 (Geneva: WHO, 2000).

61 See Jonathan M. Mann et al., "Health and Human Rights," in *Health and Human Rights: A Reader*, ed. Jonathan M. Mann et al. (New York: Routledge, 1999), 7. In the same volume, see also Rebecca Cook, "Gender, Health, and Human Rights," 262.

62 Ibid.

63 Scholtz, "International Trade Agreements," 3.

64 International Centre for Trade and Sustainable Development, "Dutch Seizure of Generic Drugs Sparks Controversy," *Bridges Weekly Trade News Digest* 13, no. 3 (January 28, 2009).

65 See International Intellectual Property Institute, *Patent Protection and Access to HIV/AIDS Pharmaceuticals in Sub-Saharan Africa* (Washington, DC: IIPI, 2000).

66 See Merrill Goozner, *The $800 Million Pill: The Truth Behind the Cost of New Drugs* (Berkeley, CA: University of California Press, 2004); and Marcia Angell, *The Truth About the Drug Companies: How They Deceive Us and What to Do About It* (New York: Random House, 2004).

67 See Inge Kaul and Ronald U. Mendoza, "Advancing the Concept of Public Goods," in *Providing Global Public Goods: Managing Globalization*, ed. Inge Kaul et al. (New York: Oxford University Press, 2003).

CHAPTER FIVE

Constructing Carbon Markets | *Learning from Experiments in the Technopolitics of Emissions Trading Schemes*

DONALD MACKENZIE

Climate change is a looming source of large-scale disaster that will require multiple kinds of interventions at multiple political scales in order to mitigate its risks. Successful intervention is a "technopolitical" matter: it must be politically viable, but it must also be materially effective, and its efficacy is a matter of its apparent detail as well as of its general features.

One of the major current initiatives for abating greenhouse-gas emissions and thus mitigating climate change risk is the development of carbon emissions markets. There is much argument about whether such an approach will be effective, but it is clear that in many contexts (such as the United States) it is more feasible politically than other measures, such as a direct carbon tax. For this reason, it is important to think carefully about how to design such markets so that they are environmentally effective. We now have a full-scale experiment that can begin to address this issue (Europe's carbon emissions market) and earlier experiments (notably the U.S. sulfur dioxide market) that are also relevant. Some lessons from these experiments are already clear: political considerations will create pressure to give away emissions allowances rather than sell them; if free allocation is chosen, then there will be pressure to allocate too many allowances; and with free allocation, emitters will make windfall profits. Those planning carbon markets cannot simply "wish away" these pressures, but they can learn from the earlier experiments, for example about the need for a powerful regulatory agency to manage the allocation process so that the pressures toward over-allocation do not weaken a carbon market to such a point that it becomes environmentally ineffective.

Perhaps the best way to illustrate how a carbon emissions market works is to begin at the local level—with my own university. All universities contain rooms and buildings that academics never enter, such as boiler houses. At my university, Edinburgh, some of the meters in these boiler houses now have two roles: as well as determining our energy bills, they measure, indirectly, our emissions of carbon dioxide. The meters have become part of the European Union Emission Trading System and thus are part of a microcosm of what may become a worldwide carbon market.

One doesn't usually think of universities as big carbon dioxide emitters, but the capacity at two of Edinburgh's three highly efficient combined heat and power centers pushes them over the 20-megawatt threshold of European emissions trading. This means that, like other operators of combustion installations of that size or larger in the EU, the university has to hold permits to emit carbon dioxide. Edinburgh University receives an allocation of allowances, each one permitting it to emit a tonne (metric ton) of carbon dioxide. If it were to emit more carbon dioxide than it has allowances for, it would have to buy extra permits on the carbon market or else face a fine. If the university were to cut its carbon emissions below its level of allowances, it could sell the excess permits, earning income from its energy frugality. Such purchases and sales take place via brokers and on a number of organized exchanges, such as Nord Pool, the Nordic power exchange. If it chose, the university could trade carbon futures—contracts that would oblige it to buy or sell allowances at a set price on a given date. Those futures are now traded on the European Climate Exchange, using the electronic trading platform of London's International Petroleum Exchange.

Edinburgh University could also indulge in more exotic trading. It could, for example, invest in a Clean Development Mechanism project in the developing world and exchange certified emission reductions from the project for European allowances. If plans for carbon trading in the

United States come to fruition and the U.S. market is linked to the European one, we could buy or sell allowances in Los Angeles or Boston. If the blueprint in the influential *Stern Review on the Economics of Climate Change*, commissioned by the U.K. Treasury, is followed globally—a big if—we will before long be able to trade carbon anywhere in the world.[1]

The science of global warming is not straightforward. The basic physics has been clear since the nineteenth century. What've been harder to understand in detail are matters such as the many feedback loops by which a rise in planetary temperature alters other processes (such as cloud formation) that affect temperature in their turn, the extent to which emissions of sulfur and particulates (which reflect sunlight) are masking greenhouse-gas warming, and the likely behavior of the great ice sheets of Antarctica and Greenland as temperatures rise. While intensive, large-scale scientific research stretching back more than thirty years has by no means eliminated all such uncertainties, its findings now point unequivocally to the conclusion that it would be dangerously irresponsible not to attempt to slow global warming. The inherent variability of the weather means that, to date, no specific, individual disaster can be attributed unequivocally to global warming, but there can be little doubt that as the process unfolds and critical thresholds are passed, the potential for weather-related disasters will increase markedly.[2]

It is broadly agreed that policy responses of two types are needed (though there is sharp disagreement as to the emphasis that should be placed on the one versus the other). First, societies must adapt to and mitigate the effects of climate change; second, the process itself must be slowed and, eventually, halted. My focus in this chapter is on the latter issue. Its relevance to this volume lies not just in the link to disaster; it is a prime site of debate over the relative roles of the state and the private sector. Governments and the international community have a variety of tools available to them to try to keep global warming to levels at which the risk of disastrous outcomes is relatively low. These include taxing greenhouse-gas emissions or imposing direct controls on them. Currently, however, policy debate is focusing on a new tool: emissions markets, such as the EU scheme. These represent a crucial shift of emphasis, in which market mechanisms play a greater role than in earlier forms of policy response to environmental dangers. However, such proposals do not replace public institutions with market mechanisms because the new market mechanisms are public institutions: they are created by deliberate government action, and, as I shall suggest, both the overall choice of a market as a tool of abatement and the design of the market are inherently political. For example, detailed investigation of the European experiment shows that slowing global warming will require careful deliberation over the details, not just the general form, of policy intervention. Market construction is technopolitical: it is simultaneously a technical and a political process.

This chapter begins by describing briefly the origins of the idea of an emissions market, which lie within economics, and discusses the first large-scale emissions market, in sulfur dioxide emissions from U.S. power stations. The fact that this market was broadly successful — in particular that there is evidence that it achieved its environmental goals more cheaply than would have been the case if direct controls had been employed — moved emissions markets decisively into the policy mainstream, first in the United States and then more broadly. After touching on the Kyoto Protocol, which was strongly influenced by U.S. enthusiasm for emissions trading, the chapter then focuses on the EU scheme, currently the world's most important carbon market. The scheme covers around two billion tonnes of carbon dioxide emissions a year — about half Europe's total emissions — and in 2008 European carbon trades totaled $91.9 billion.[3]

The remaining sections of the chapter deal with lessons that can be learned from the experience to date of the European market. Its construction was a remarkable achievement, but one marred, at least in its first phase (2005–7), by over-allocation of emission allowances and by windfall profits earned by big emitters, in particular electricity suppliers. Avoiding such mistakes is essential, I would argue, when considering how a nationwide carbon market in the United States — and perhaps eventually a global carbon market — can best be constructed. Carbon markets are only one tool in the struggle to slow climate change, but they can be a useful one — if they are properly designed.

TRADING EMISSIONS

The debate about how best to slow global warming is one largely dominated by economists. They tend to be skeptical about both voluntary restraint and the capacity of governments to find cost-effective ways of directly curbing emissions. The record so far suggests they may be right on the former. The profession in general is perhaps too pessimistic about a direct role for government, but while there's clearly a need for greatly increased government funding for R&D (research and development), it's certainly true that government intervention in the field of energy technology has had at best mixed results, as the checkered history of nuclear power demonstrates. Instead, economists have tended to support mechanisms that curb emissions of carbon dioxide and other greenhouse gases (which have up to now been "free," from the viewpoint of the emitter) by making them carry a price. A carbon tax could do that, but in recent years the proposed mechanism has often tended to be a "cap-and-trade" scheme, such as the one now in place in Europe.

In such schemes governments set a cap on emissions, sell or give that number of allowances to emitters, and then monitor emissions and fine emitters that exceed their allowances. If the monitoring and penalties are stringent enough, overall emissions will be kept down to the level of the cap. Those for whom reduction is expensive will want to buy allowances rather than incur disproportionate costs. The supply of allowances is created by the financial incentive thereby provided to those who can make big cuts in emissions relatively cheaply. They can save money by not having to buy allowances or (if allowances are distributed for free) earn money by selling allowances they don't need.

The idea of controlling emissions via a cap-and-trade scheme was first put forward in detail in 1968 by the University of Toronto economist J. H. Dales.[4] Emissions markets were implemented in relatively minor and sometimes ham-fisted ways in the 1970s and 1980s, mainly in the United States. It was only in the 1990s that the idea became mainstream. The crucial development was the start of sulfur dioxide trading in the United States in 1995. It had been known for twenty years or more that damage to the environment and to human health was being caused by sulfur dioxide emissions, notably from coal-fired power stations, which react in the atmosphere to produce acid rain and other acid depositions. Numerous bills were presented to Congress in the 1980s to address the problem, but all failed in the face of opposition from the Reagan administration and from Democrats who represented states that might suffer economically from controls, such as the areas of Appalachia and the Midwest in which coal deposits are high in sulfur.

Sulfur trading was a way round the impasse. It combined a clear goal that environmentalists could embrace (cutting annual sulfur dioxide emissions from U.S. power stations by ten million tons from their 1980 level, a reduction of around half) with a market mechanism attractive to at least some Republicans. A particularly influential lobbyist for trading was the advocacy group Environmental Defense. One of its staff members, the lawyer Joe Goffman, largely drafted Title IV of the Clean Air Act Amendments of 1990, which introduced sulfur dioxide trading. Economists, such as MIT's Richard Schmalensee and Robert Stavins of Harvard's Kennedy School, also became involved. They didn't simply advocate a cap-and-trade scheme, but helped it gain political acceptance.

The 1990 legislation differed from what economists might have wanted in two respects. First, there was no attempt at a cost-benefit analysis to determine the optimum level of reduction of sulfur dioxide emissions — and in a sense fortunately so. Cost-benefit analyses of contentious issues tend simply to become mired in controversy because they often pivot on factors that can only be estimated, not measured. (Combating global climate change involves costs incurred and benefits experienced at different points in time, and weighing up the balance between costs and benefits involves choice of the "discount rate" that is used, for example, to work out the present dollar value of a cost incurred several decades from now. That discount rate often turns out to be arithmetically the dominant factor in the cost-benefit calculation. There has already been fierce technical dispute over the *Stern Review*'s choice of a low discount rate and thus high present-day values.) A ten-million-ton reduction in sulfur dioxide emissions was essentially a compromise between environmentalist demands for a cut of twelve million tons and industry proposals for eight million, and the economists involved simply accepted it.[5]

Second, when economists, such as Dales, proposed emissions trading, they assumed that governments would sell allowances. Instead, nearly all the sulfur allowances were given away free of charge to the utility companies that operated power stations, in amounts roughly (but, as discussed below, not exactly) proportional to the calorific value of the fuel they burned in the baseline years 1985–87. Any economist can readily tell you why "grandfathering" — as this is called — isn't usually the optimum way of proceeding. It entrenches incumbents because of the cost advantage they enjoy over newcomers, who have to pay for their allowances. Indeed, if an industry can see grandfathering coming, there's an incentive to increase a polluting activity in order to achieve a larger allocation. Grandfathering can also increase social inequality. For reasons discussed below, industries can be expected to increase their prices to take account of the market value of carbon allowances, even if they have received them free of charge. This will benefit shareholders (who are usually amongst the better off) but disadvantage consumers (who often aren't).[6]

Those who planned the sulfur dioxide market realized, however, that there was no politically feasible alternative to the free distribution of allowances. Forcing utility companies to buy them would have generated a fatal level of hostility from the industry, but giving them away meant enormously complex jostling over the rules. In the months leading up to the eventual signing of the bill by President Bush on November 15, 1990, there was intense lobbying for provisions that would favor mining and/or utility interests in particular states by introducing exceptions to the baseline allocation of 2.5 lb. of sulfur dioxide per million British thermal units of input. Some states, such as Florida, won favorable allocations because they were expected to be finely balanced in that autumn's elections.

For some of the economists involved in the sulfur market, it was an education in the political process. Schmalensee—co-author of the best study of the market[7]—recalls laughing when a special provision for lignite, the low-grade brown coal common in North Dakota, was proposed at a meeting of Congressional staff members at which he was present. He was "forcefully reminded that North Dakota was a relatively poor state with bleak prospects and, more important, that Chairman Burdick"—Quentin Burdick, the octogenarian Democrat from North Dakota who chaired the Senate Committee on Environment and Public Works—"was not to be trifled with."[8] The lignite provision duly became law.

Uncorrected, the need to buy off potential Congressional opposition would have resulted in a failure to achieve the ten-million-ton reduction. When the implications of all the various exemptions, such as the lignite provision, were worked out (not a simple task), they added up to an over-allocation of allowances of around 10%. Those lobbying for the legislation had, however, cleverly inserted a correction mechanism early in the legislative process: "the ratchet," as it became known. This clawed back any aggregate over-allocation by imposing a corresponding across-the-board cut in allowances. Once the more powerful special interests had successfully been bought off with what turned out to be the 10% over-allocation, everyone's allocation was reduced by roughly a tenth. The detailed calculations were made not by the House or the Senate but by the Environmental Protection Agency, which imposed the ratchet months after the legislation was irrevocably on the statute books. The sheer complication of working out what the rules implied for the sizes of allocations hampered opposition to the ratchet: participants seem to have assumed that it would cut their allocations by only around a twentieth.

While all the politicking affected who got what, the ratchet kept the requisite overall cut in emissions more or less intact. Furthermore, the cut was then achieved far more cheaply than almost anyone had imagined. Industry lobbyists had claimed it would cost $10 billion a year; the actual cost was around $1 billion. Allowance prices of $400 a ton were predicted, but in fact prices averaged around $150 or less in the early years of the scheme. The flexibility that the market gave to utilities helped reduce costs by around half compared to a more directive approach (in which, for example, all plants would have had to meet a uniform maximum emissions rate), but factors other than trading also kept costs down.[9] "Scrubbers" to remove sulfur from smokestacks turned out to be cheaper to install and to run than had been anticipated, and rail-freight deregulation sharply reduced the cost of transportation from Wyoming's Powder River Basin, the main source of low-sulfur coal in the United States.

KYOTO AND BEYOND

That the sulfur dioxide market was, broadly, a success shaped the way the Clinton administration approached the negotiations that led to the 1997 Kyoto Protocol. In the protocol, the industrialized nations undertook that by Kyoto's 2008–12 "commitment period" they would have limited their greenhouse-gas emissions to agreed proportions of their 1990 levels: 93% for the United States, 92% for the European Union (with varying levels for its member states), and so on.

At the insistence of the United States, Kyoto gave its signatories flexibility in how to meet their commitments. A country with a Kyoto commitment can meet it by controlling emissions domestically. Alternatively, it can pay for abatement made via projects in developing countries that don't have Kyoto targets (the Clean Development Mechanism) or via projects in other industrialized countries (these Joint Implementation projects are mainly to be found in the former Soviet bloc). Indeed, a nation-state signatory can simply pay another signatory for reductions the latter has made beyond its commitments. Because the Kyoto commitments of Russia and other countries in the former Soviet bloc did not take into account the collapse of heavy industry after the fall of communism, they have a lot of essentially spurious "reductions" to sell once their governments have met the requirements for international trading under Kyoto.

The Kyoto Protocol was no more than the barest skeleton of a market, containing almost no detail on how trading was to take place. The United States had only just got its way. Much of the developing world was suspicious of international trading as likely "carbon colonialism," fearing that the developed world would use it to escape its responsibilities. Notoriously, the United States then walked away. In March 2001, the Bush administration announced that the United States was pulling out of the Kyoto Protocol.

The EU had wanted a mixture of harmonized carbon taxes and coordinated government measures to promote low-carbon technologies, but by 2001 the idea of carbon trading had come into favor in Europe. In part prompted by lobbying by Environmental Defense, the oil company BP had set up an internal carbon-trading scheme between its business units. While no cash actually changed hands, attention was given to cutting emissions. BP was able quickly to meet its 10% target and even made money doing it by saving on energy costs and selling natural gas that would previously have been vented or flared. The favorable outcome was influential, but what was less widely noticed at the time was that BP discovered that the initial allowance allocations to its business units were too generous: in particular they were based on over-optimistic projections of growth. The scheme was given "teeth" only by making allocations in the scheme's second year much tighter than in its first.[10]

Denmark launched a carbon market among its big electricity producers in 2001. The United Kingdom began an experimental voluntary scheme in 2002. The incentive to participate in the latter was a government subsidy in return for a promised emissions reduction. As with the BP scheme, however, participants in the U.K. scheme found they could easily meet the targets they had taken on. With allowances thus in surplus, prices were low and trading essentially dried up.

THE EUROPEAN UNION EMISSION TRADING SYSTEM

The landmark European scheme has been the EU's carbon market, launched in January 2005.[11] Europe moved toward trading rather than the initially preferred carbon tax in good part because of an idiosyncratic feature of the EU's political procedures. Tax measures require unanimity: a single dissenting country can block them. Emissions trading, however, counts as an environmental matter, which takes it into the terrain of "qualified majority voting." No single country can stop such a scheme: to do so a coalition of countries would have to form a "blocking minority" (voting weights roughly follow population). A plan for a Europe-wide carbon tax had foundered in the early 1990s in the face of vehement opposition from industry and from particular member states (notably the U.K.), and its advocates knew that if they tried to revive it the unanimity rule meant they were unlikely to succeed. "We learned our lesson," one of them told me. Hence the shift to trading.

In the United States, there is a similar political difficulty in establishing a carbon tax; and so the lessons of Europe are relevant in considering possible U.S. carbon emission reduction schemes. The design of the European trading scheme was deliberately simple. To date, it covers only carbon dioxide and does not include other greenhouse gases, such as methane. In sulfur trading in the United States, each smokestack is fitted with automatic measurement devices. European carbon dioxide emissions are measured less directly, using the method known as "mass balance," in which gas-meter readings or invoiced quantities of coal or oil, for example, are multiplied by appropriate emission and oxidation factors. Only large, fixed installations are covered. Ground transport and shipping are omitted, aviation has yet to be brought into the market, and the domestic sector is covered only indirectly via the participation of electricity suppliers. In consequence, no more than half of Europe's emissions currently fall within the scheme.

The European carbon market is nevertheless a remarkable achievement. It took the United States five years from legislation passage to begin sulfur trading; the EU developed what was in many ways a more difficult market in three years. The number of big emitters of carbon dioxide is larger than that of big producers of sulfur dioxide, and the EU has also been in the throes of expansion. The tricky technical stuff that too often undermines ambitious government programs—such as constructing the central database and national registries and keeping track of the allocation of allowances to thousands of installations—went on the whole remarkably well.

The trading of allowances seems to be going smoothly, with only limited technical disruptions even when the market is extremely busy. (The main exception has been the discovery in 2009 that there were cases in which the scheme was being used for a form of tax fraud, and clamping down on the fraud has required changes in the tax rules governing allowance trading.) Measurement and independent verification, the foundations of any emissions market, are improving. There were a lot of difficulties in 2005, the first year of the scheme, simply as a result of companies' unfamiliarity with what they had to do, but later measurements are better in that respect.

Inconsistencies across Europe in relation to the interpretation of measurement rules remain a problem, and there is some room for "gaming." Installations can choose to use either the standard emission factor for a type of fuel or a factor specific to the particular fuel they are using. If an installation burns coal with a carbon content higher than that assumed by the standard factor while using that factor to calculate emissions, it can deliberately underestimate its emissions, perhaps by around 2%. This doesn't sound like a lot, but aggregated over the scheme it could have a significant impact on the balance between the supply and demand for allowances. Apparent little details, such as how the carbon content of coal is measured, can affect how effective a carbon emissions market is.

OVER-ALLOCATION

Even at the start of the European scheme, however, there was reason to be optimistic that, with careful attention, measurement problems of this kind were tractable, given that the market covered only big emissions of a single gas, carbon dioxide (and did not include, for example, the absorption of carbon dioxide by the biosphere, which is much harder to measure). Two larger difficulties, however, remained. One was the politics of allocation. In the first phase of the Emission Trading System (from January 2005 to December 2007), Europe did not find its equivalent of the ratchet. As with sulfur, almost all carbon allowances have so far been given away, not auctioned. Again, the scheme's designers felt that this was the only feasible way to proceed, fearing in particular that the similarity of the revenue-generating aspect of an auction to a tax might mean that the scheme would require the unanimous vote of EU member states after all.

The amounts of the allowances are governed by National Allocation Plans drawn up by each member state. Predictably, Europe's industries and most of its governments pressed for generous allowances. The European Commission rejected the most outrageous of the plans for the 2005–7 phase, demanding a 25% cut in Slovakia's plan and a 16.5% cut in Poland's. However, smaller exaggerations in the majority of national plans added up to a scheme that in the first phase was in overall surplus.

Initially, the extent of over-allocation wasn't clear. As the price of natural gas rose relative to that of coal in 2005 and the early months of 2006, so did the price of the allowances needed to burn coal, which is much more carbon-intensive than natural gas. Market participants also had to worry about such uncertainties as the weather: a serious cold snap should push the carbon price up, as should a prolonged dry spell (because it reduces hydroelectric capacity).

Europe's power sector was in general short of allowances, while the excess was concentrated in the hands of energy-intensive industry. The big power generators are experienced, active traders, who often sell electricity at prices fixed a year or so in advance and thus want to hedge the risk of big rises in the costs of their inputs, which now include carbon allowances. This meant that they wanted to buy allowances, but industrial companies (often without an equivalent tradition of trading) were slow to sell, preferring to wait and see the extent to which their emissions fell short of their allocations.

The resultant temporary imbalance of supply and demand caused prices to rise markedly from January 2005 to March 2006, peaking at €31/tonne (that is, around $40 per tonne, or per 1,000 kg of carbon dioxide), a level that, if it had been sustained, would probably have been a sufficient incentive to encourage real emissions reductions. In April and May 2006, however, the news gradually leaked out that in 2005 the industries and power generators of most of the EU's member states had produced less carbon dioxide than their national allocations. On April 26, 2006, the European carbon price fell 30%, and by mid May allowances were trading as low as €9. As the fact of over-allocation sunk in, prices fell almost to zero: by the end of the 2005–7 phase, one could buy the right to emit a tonne of carbon dioxide for as little as €0.04, little more than a thousandth of the peak price.

Despite the over-allocation and price crash, the European trading scheme probably did lead to some modest abatement even in its first phase. The carbon price was high enough, some of the time, to prompt electricity generators to use plants fueled by natural gas rather than coal-fired plants, and the very act of measuring emissions may have focused attention on how they could be cut. One study, for example, suggests that total 2005 emissions from the sectors covered by the scheme were around 7% lower than would have been predicted simply by extrapolating pre-2005 emissions in the light of economic growth and the trend in carbon intensity in European economies,[12] though that could be an overestimate because pre-2005 figures are much less reliable than more recent data: one effect of the scheme has been better knowledge of emission patterns.

There's a sense, furthermore, in which the first phase of the European scheme was always meant as an experiment rather than as a tool to deliver substantial emissions reductions. The second phase, which runs from January 2008 until the end of the Kyoto commitment period in December 2012, is more significant. The European Commission saw the need to ensure the credibility of what is in many ways its flagship policy. That the scheme involves systematic measurement of carbon dioxide emissions at the plant level means that the Commission also now has much better data to use to evaluate National Allocation Plans, and the fact that the second phase of trading coincides with the Kyoto commitment period means that there's a clear benchmark against which to assess the plans of all the countries that are in danger of not meeting their Kyoto commitments. So the second time round the Commission was significantly tougher in its assessments. Once again almost all member states sought over-generous allocations, but their wishes weren't granted: all but four of the twenty-seven member states' plans were rejected.

What at the start of this chapter I called the "technopolitics" of carbon dioxide in Europe has shifted. The Commission, in effect, imposed a formula on the member states (the so-called NAP formula: NAPs are National Allocation Plans), turning what had originally been a process involving extensive behind-the-scenes negotiation into something more technocratic. The formula is that a country's annual average allocation for 2008–12 is:

(2005 emissions) × (GDP growth factor) × (carbon intensity improvement)

Crucially, the second and third factors—which could easily be "fudged"— are not member-state estimates but determined by the European Commission using PRIMES, an economic model of the European energy market.

What permitted the technopolitical shift was above all the very existence of the Emission Trading System: both the emissions data it has generated and the way it has become an established feature of the European political landscape. One of the scheme's designers told me in an interview that in the run-up to the scheme's first phase they had to be very cautious: if they had been too stringent with too many member states, it was all too easy to imagine a European summit deciding to postpone the scheme, perhaps indefinitely. In contrast, the allocations for the second phase took place in what the interviewee called "a completely different context": "Feasibility, data availability... Facts are in place. One is that the emissions trading [scheme] is there, and the idea of it ever not being there is not on the agenda and would shock the political process." That does not mean, however, that carbon-market politics in Europe is at an end, because a number of countries unhappy with the cuts imposed by the Commission have taken legal action against it. On September 23, 2009, Europe's second-highest tribunal, the Court of First Instance, annulled the Commission's decisions in respect to the caps it imposed on Poland and Estonia, concluding that the Commission had exceeded its powers. The decision (which the Commission will almost certainly appeal) threatens to return the European carbon market to the earlier situation in which political exigencies produced over-allocation.

The global recession that began in the fall of 2008 has of course also had an impact on the European carbon market. As industrial activity falls, emissions fall with it, so the price of allowances has decreased sharply, roughly halving between June 2008 and May 2009. So far, though, the fall has not been to zero or anything close to it: at the time of writing in October 2009, the price of European allowances is around €13 (about $18) per tonne. The fact that allowances can be "banked" into the scheme's third phase (2013–20) has helped keep prices up, and the current price — while not sufficient to encourage substantial investments in mitigation — at least keeps the issue of emissions a live one as corporate decisionmakers deal with the economic downturn.

WINDFALL PROFITS

The second major problem to afflict the European Union Emission Trading System is the windfall profits made by the most important sector covered by the scheme, electricity generators, as a result of receiving most of their allowances free of charge. Just as an economist would predict, the electricity generators have raised their prices to take account of the value of these allowances. (A profit-maximizing firm will produce electricity only if its price is such that what the firm can earn by doing so is more than it would earn by not doing so, and the latter calculation now includes what it could earn by selling carbon emissions allowances it would no longer need.) Thus the United Kingdom's energy regulator Ofgem (the Office of the Gas and Electricity Markets) calculated that in January 2008 the cost of carbon dioxide allowances made up around 17% of electricity's wholesale price in the United Kingdom and that the 2008–12 phase of the Emission Trading System would increase generators' profits by a total of around $17 billion.[13]

The cure for windfall profits is for governments to auction allowances rather than distribute them for free: the price of electricity and other carbon dioxide–intensive products will still go up, but the auction revenues are available to governments and can, for example, be used in programs to promote energy efficiency and combat fuel poverty. The shape that the Emission Trading System will take in its third phase, which will begin in 2013, is not yet entirely clear, but it now seems likely that — at least in sectors, such as electricity, that face limited competition from outside the European Union — auctioning will largely replace free allocation. Such a move would have been far too ambitious politically before the trading scheme was established but is now feasible.

CONCLUSION

The technopolitics of carbon markets runs deeper than the issues of over-allocation and windfall profits on which I have focused. The European Union Emission Trading System is, in relative terms, simple. As noted, it covers so far only carbon dioxide, not the other greenhouse gases, and only large stationary sources; it also encompasses a bloc of countries with an established procedure for making decisions on matters that affect them all. Even it, though, raises complex issues that I have been unable to cover here, such as how to incorporate carbon allowances into companies' financial reporting[14] and how to minimize "leakage" (shifts in the production of carbon-intensive goods, such as steel and cement, to outside the boundaries of an emissions market). Move beyond carbon dioxide to the other greenhouse gases or to "sinks" (biosphere features, such as tropical forests, that absorb carbon dioxide) as well as sources of carbon dioxide, and measurement problems multiply. Try to include shipping or aviation, and political difficulties increase: the EU seems headed for a court battle with the international airlines, especially those of the United States, over the legitimacy of including flights other than those internal to the EU in the Emission Trading System. Move beyond a partially unified political system, such as the EU, to the international level, and problems deepen even further. The Kyoto Protocol's Clean Development Mechanism, for example, is fully international, includes all the greenhouse gases covered by the Protocol, and (at least potentially) encompasses sinks, such as forests, as well as sources. It has had a difficult and contentious history, which unfortunately cannot be discussed here for reasons of space.[15]

In the face of a multiplicity of daunting issues it would be easy to dismiss attempts to construct environmentally effective carbon markets as futile. The political exigencies of establishing cap-and-trade markets can, for example, be expected always to lead to the temptation to allocate permits to incumbents free of charge rather than face the industry opposition that auctioning engenders and always to involve strong pressures toward over-allocation of these free allowances. The reason, however,

I have drawn attention to sulfur's ratchet and the European Commission's NAP formula is two-fold. First, they demonstrate that the politics of emissions markets is indeed technopolitics: they are detailed technical devices but serve a political purpose, which is to prevent the markets of which they are part from being rendered pointless by over-allocation of allowances. Second, the success of the ratchet and what appears (at least until the unexpected court ruling and the unanticipated sharp recession came into play) to have been the success of the NAP formula show that the predictable pressure toward over-allocation need not triumph, even in situations in which auctioning is politically infeasible. The sulfur dioxide market did, broadly speaking, work; the European carbon market has shown encouraging signs of starting to do so. As other countries (such as the United States) design carbon markets, they will have to find their equivalents of the ratchet or the NAP formula, and most likely there will have to be a powerful regulator akin to the European Commission to ensure that the application of such devices is not subverted by vested interests.

It is, of course, also necessary to point out that carbon markets can be expected to be at most only one instrument of abatement. The many subsidies that the extraction and use of fossil fuels still enjoy worldwide need to be withdrawn (though in some contexts, difficult problems to do with fuel poverty will need to be solved first). Taxes and direct technological standards, such as maximum emission levels for motor vehicles and perhaps even for power stations, still have major parts to play. Why, for example, should aviation continue to enjoy an advantage over other forms of travel because its fuel isn't taxed while theirs often is? Levels of public investment in research and development on low-carbon technologies and on other ways of mitigating global warming are absurdly low. Governments, not markets, may have to take the lead in the bigger tasks, such as refashioning electricity grids so that the best use can be made of the full range of renewable sources. In the struggle against climate change, humanity needs all the tools we can lay our hands on. As I have emphasized, carbon markets are only one of these, but if pitfalls of the kind discussed here can be avoided, they can play a helpful role in meeting one of the greatest challenges we face.

NOTES

1 Nicholas Stern, *The Economics of Climate Change: The Stern Review* (Cambridge: Cambridge University Press, 2007).

2 See, for example, Hans Joachim Schellnhuber et al., eds., *Avoiding Dangerous Climate Change* (Cambridge: Cambridge University Press, 2006).

3 Karan Capoor and Philippe Ambrosi, *State and Trends of the Carbon Market 2009* (Washington, DC: World Bank, 2009), 1.

4 John Harkness Dales, *Pollution, Property and Prices: An Essay in Policy-Making and Economics* (Toronto: University of Toronto Press, 1968).

5 Robert N. Stavins, "What Can We Learn from the Grand Policy Experiment? Lessons from SO2 Allowance Trading," *Journal of Economic Perspectives* 12, no. 3 (Summer 1998): 69–88; and Dallas Burtraw et al., "Economics of Pollution Trading for SO_2 and NO_X," *Annual Review of Environment and Resources* 30 (November 2005): 253–89.

6 Ian W. H. Parry, "Are Emissions Permits Regressive?" *Journal of Environmental Economics and Management* 47, no. 2 (March 2004): 364–87.

7 The discussion of the sulfur dioxide market in this, the previous paragraph, and the following two paragraphs draws heavily on this study: A. Denny Ellerman et al., *Markets for Clean Air: The U.S. Acid Rain Program* (Cambridge: Cambridge University Press, 2000).

8 Ibid., 46.

9 For a review of studies of the extent to which the sulfur dioxide market saved costs, see Burtraw et al., "Economics of Pollution Trading," 263–65.

10 David G. Victor and Joshua C. House, "BP's Emissions Trading System," *Energy Policy* 34, no. 15 (October 2006): 2100–2112.

11 My discussion of the European Union Emission Trading System is based upon twenty-five interviews with carbon-market participants (including traders, brokers, market designers, and members of NGOs seeking to influence market design) and observations of two major market meetings, Point Carbon's Carbon Market Insights conferences in 2007 and 2008. Those seeking further information on the development of the scheme should turn to Jos Delbeke, ed., *EU Environmental Law: The EU Greenhouse Gas Emissions Trading Scheme*, vol. 4, *EU Energy Law* (Leuven, Belgium: Claeys and Casteels, 2006); A. Denny Ellerman, Barbara K. Buchner, and Carlo Carraro, *Allocation in the European Emissions Trading Scheme: Rights, Rents and Fairness* (Cambridge: Cambridge University Press, 2007); and Jon Birger Skjærseth and Jørgen Wettestad, *EU Emissions Trading: Initiation, Decision-making and Implementation* (Aldershot, UK: Ashgate, 2008).

12 A. Denny Ellerman and Barbara K. Buchner, "The European Union Emissions Trading Scheme: Origins, Allocation, and Early Results," *Review of Environmental Economics and Policy* 1, no. 1 (2007): 66–87.

13 Ed Crooks, "Watchdog Wants £9bn Windfall Electricity Profits Clawed Back," *Financial Times*, January 17, 2008. U.K. electricity generators contest the accuracy of these figures.

14 See Donald MacKenzie, "Making Things the Same: Gases, Emission Rights and the Politics of Carbon Markets," *Accounting, Organizations and Society* 34 (2009): 440–55.

15 A useful source on the wider problems of carbon trading is Larry Lohmann, ed., "Carbon Trading: A Critical Conversation on Climate Change, Privatisation and Power," *Development Dialogue*, no. 48 (September 2006).

Contributors

SHEILA JASANOFF is Pforzheimer Professor of Science and Technology Studies at the Harvard Kennedy School. She has authored more than 100 publications on the role of science and technology in the law, politics, and public policy of modern democracies, with particular focus on the regulation of biotechnology and the environment in the U.S., Europe, and India.

HEINZ KLUG is Evjue-Bascom Professor in Law at the University of Wisconsin and Senior Honorary Research Fellow at the University of the Witwatersrand. He is also director of Global Legal Studies at the University of Wisconsin Law School. He is the author of *Constituting Democracy: Law, Globalism and Political Reconstruction in South Africa* (Cambridge University Press, 2000).

ANDREW LAKOFF is associate professor of anthropology, sociology, and communication at the University of Southern California. He is the author of *Pharmaceutical Reason: Knowledge and Value in Global Psychiatry* (Cambridge University Press, 2005) and co-editor of *Biosecurity Interventions: Global Health and Security in Question* (Columbia University Press/SSRC Books, 2008).

DONALD MACKENZIE holds a personal chair in sociology at the University of Edinburgh. His most recent book is *Material Markets: How Economic Agents are Constructed* (Oxford University Press, 2009).

PATRICK S. ROBERTS is an assistant professor in the Center for Public Administration and Policy in the School of Public and International Affairs at Virginia Tech. He has published articles in scholarly and popular journals on disaster and security organizations and on political executives in the United States.

P. W. SINGER is director of the 21st Century Defense Initiative at the Brookings Institution. His latest book is *Wired for War: The Robotics Revolution and Conflict in the 21st Century* (Penguin, 2009).